Too Many Masks

~

and The Anger Within

by James T Petra

(Learn how one man healed his child within to break his cycle of abuse. Get a look into what motivates the cycle of child abuse. Learn the truth about Anger. Learn how thinking and feeling better about yourself will help you stop hurting other people. Gain strength in reading affirmations to replace the negative self-talk that keep you from progressing in your recovery and help you stay victim free.)

The stories in this book attempt to reflect the thoughts, feelings, experiences, and circumstances expressed by the author. Most of the names, locales, and identifying details have been changed to protect victims and those who are still wearing *Too Many Masks*.

Printed on recycled, acid-free paper that meets the American National Standards Institute Z39.48 Standard

Cover picture 'Little Sad Clown2' by iGabo © iGabo.deviantart.com
Gustavo A Ricart / Dominican Republic

Dedications

*To my wife Tara, who has taught me that love does not consist in gazing at each other, but in looking outward together in the same direction.
*To my spiritual family, for much love and support in spite of myself.
*To Betty (Dotty), who has worked arduously in turning my chicken scratch handwriting into her computer program, this was quite the chore. But most importantly, thank you from the bottom of my heart for being the BEST spiritual MOM I have ever known.
*To Ed A.K Jr. :o) from the beginning of this project, many thanks my friend.
*To my brother Jerry, who has been an invaluable support and strength. I will always be proud of you, I have no idea how you developed your good parenting skills.
*To The Centers of Behavioral Health PTSD Services for restoring peoples Safety, Trust, Power/Control, Esteem and Intimacy in Humanity and Oneself. *To the understaffed, underfunded, and underappreciated Abuse Treatment Centers, Deviant Criminal Behavioral and Recovery Programs making public and private contributions stretch while succeeding in keeping our dysfunctional family members on the right track.
*To the many who are in a treatment program, whether a victim or a perpetrator or both. This book is for you, there is hope, and there is recovery… to new beginnings together.

(Because the last is often remembered, more than anything else is.)
*Most importantly, this book is dedicated to my victims / which includes the ones left picking up the pieces, to all victims of abuse.

*This book was made in part because of the ones that would not listen, and have judged without knowing the whole story, for those that continue to wear

TOO MANY MASKS.

TABLE OF CONTENTS

-FOREWORD-

You may have noticed this book because of the cover that pulls you in, or perhaps you or someone you know experienced some form of trauma or abuse. There is a growing awareness of the prevalence of trauma in our society. This book provides witness to one man's experiences. James Petra found some initial healing through telling his story in this book, but later he found a more thorough healing after he sought treatment specific to Post Traumatic Stress Disorder while working with a therapist trained in Cognitive Processing Therapy. James had explained that until he could examine those areas of his life he was trying so hard to forget, and look at them realistically, he could not change his own destructive behaviors.

When a person, especially a child, experiences trauma, they try to make sense of something that is often senseless. Without supports and other means of reasoning, many times the person will take on the blame for the incident, even very extreme abuse. This becomes so painful that avoidance – trying to believe it did not happen / that they really weren't affected by the abuse, or trying to block memories is next. Trauma can become all consuming, popping up and influencing our choices and behaviors in life, until you are able to look at the trauma realistically, in a structured and safe manner, allowing the natural emotions to be experienced.

James felt compelled to show a good face despite all the evidence to the contrary. In order for James to move past denial and stop his cycle of abuse he had to peel off the many "masks" he developed in order to survive.

If you, or someone you know, have experienced abuse that was so significant that it continues to interrupt or cause problems in your life, I strongly encourage you to seek out a professional psychotherapist trained to fully evaluate your situation. Then I would recommend that you ask to be provided with one of the three evidence based psychotherapy treatments for trauma / PTSD (Post Traumatic Stress Disorder).

These three therapies are

1) Prolonged Exposure,

2) Cognitive Processing Therapy, or

3) EMDR (Eye Movement Desensitization and Reprocessing).

For anyone wanting more information, please contact your local PTSD Treatment Services nearest you.

~Doing this honest hard work is the kindest thing you could do for yourself.~

AUTHORS NOTES

My hope in writing this book was to accomplish many things, most of which are brought out in the introduction section. I also wanted to reach as many people as possible with an important point: Abusive behavior comes in many forms and the victims that are affected from its catastrophic wake are endless. By sharing my life story, I hope to reach not only perpetrators of abuse, but also the innocent victims who were personally violated.

No matter what you have done that seemed to look as if you had caused the crime against you. That is the farthest from the truth. *You were powerless and not at all to blame.* If you are a secondary victim, whether a relative of the victim or of the perpetrator, *you were powerless* too. The perpetrator of abuse spends an enormous amount of time and resources covering his tracks and setting up the next move on his victim(s).

By reading this book, you will undoubtedly learn that if children do not have a healthy relationship with their parent(s) or guardian(s) and if adults do not learn to listen to their intuitions, then the cycle of abuse will continue.

Adult children of abuse *must* get help; we cannot break this cycle on our own. Keeping the abuse quiet only strengthens the perpetrator and continues to put you working for them. Please, I urge anyone who reads this to get the help you need and deserve.

We can stop the cycle of abuse, one voice at a time

One last note: I must warn you this is not an easy read. It's very descriptive and sometimes way too much information. For example, I debated a long time whether to edit the bad language or to leave it in. Personally, I don't pick up novels that use profanity, but then again this book is a true story therefore sugar coating the real life dysfunction would be minimizing my toxic life. So I do hope you can see your way through this book in spite of my candor.

Like most books on this topic, we all need to seek ways to protect our children from all types of abuse in real life, let alone have them read it. By reading books like these ourselves, we can learn the tools to teach our children.

~ **GROUNDING** is at the end of this book. ~

If you find yourself having trouble reading this book because of the content, especially if you yourself have experienced trauma in YOUR history, please review the last two pages of this book. If at any time you are overwhelmed with emotional pain, you may need a way to detach so that you can gain control over your feelings and stay safe. **Grounding** "anchors" you to the present and to reality.

Because of the above-mentioned reasons, I would strongly encourage anyone who is a victim of abuse to read this book in conjunction with therapy.

INTRODUCTION

"YOU ARE ONLY AS SICK AS YOUR SECRETS."

I have learned many things during my recovery that I wished I had known before things in my life got so crazy. During my recovery, I have come to believe whole-heartedly the above-mentioned affirmation, "You are only as sick as your secrets." Until now, I have been carrying too many secrets with me for far too long. Thus, I have led a very sick and destructive life.

At one time or another, we put on some type of "mask" while going through life. The problems come about when we wear so many masks that we start to forget who we really are. Perhaps you would rather not know the real you. On the other hand, maybe you do not feel worthy of getting to know yourself, so you fake it the best way you know how. However, I can speak from experience; "Beware, if you have *TOO MANY MASKS*." You will get up one day and say to yourself, "Who am I today?" and you truly won't be able to answer that question.

In the book, entitled 'Facing Co-dependence' Pia Melody writes the following: "The secret to your recovery is to learn to embrace your own history. Look at it, become aware of it, and experience your feelings about the less-than-nurturing events of your past. Because if you do not, the issues from your history will be held in minimization, denial and delusion and truly be behind you as demons you are not aware of. In addition, this situation will continue to make you miserable through your own dysfunctional behaviors.

More directly, I tell my patients 'Hug your demons or they will bite you in the ass.' In other words, 'If you do not embrace what is dysfunctional, you are doomed to repeat it and stay in the pain.' "

My sincere hope is that by reading this book, somehow my own journey will help you find the road to healing your trauma and recovery.

This book is about my life, in chronological order, to show people that a person just does not wake up one day and decide to abuse or act destructively. As a child, I suffered from physical, emotional, and sexual abuse. By sharing my life experience with you, my aim is to expose my personal caustic cycle of destructive thoughts and feelings that led to my own abusive behavior. Perhaps this will help you to identify your own destructive actions, or those of someone close to you, that has *chosen* a similar path in life. I say chosen because, as you will see by the time you finish reading this book, that for every action we take there is first a thought process, thus a choice is made.

If we allow the blame game or pride to stand in our way from wholeheartedly trying to stop the shamefully toxic view of ourselves and if we refuse to get the help that we so desperately need to stop the cycle of abuse, then we will continue to stay stuck and out of control. We *cannot* break this lifelong cycle of abuse *alone*. I have tried and failed miserably as you will soon see through the pages of this book.

"I have been amazed to see that, in sharing my secrets,

others can identify with me."

~John Bradshaw 'Home Coming'

By sharing my secrets, I hope you will discover that no matter what the type or degree of abuse that you have suffered through or inflicted upon your victims, you are not a "lost cause."

Remember, it is *never* too late to change. There is a time for everything and the time to heal is now! No matter what our history, the future can bring about positive changes. We can regain self-respect and self-forgiveness, and even perhaps regain some of that dignity we seemed to have lost along the way.

Once we mend ourselves from within, we begin to understand why we made the poor choices that perpetuate the cycle of abuse.

The opportunity is before you to acquire the tools for positive change. I am not proud of my involvement in abusing, but if my experience can help at least one person and if by exposing all of the shame-filled dysfunctional Masks I have worn throughout my life, and if one child is saved from what I went through then this is all worth it. I have vowed that the cycle of abuse stop with me. If I can choose to change then so can you. However, we cannot change two things.

Our history and

The individuals who wronged us.

Nevertheless, we can change ourselves by stopping the cycle of abuse and thus make our homes and our communities safe from all types of abuse.

*Healing from trauma and recovery is not about blame, it is about taking responsibility for our own actions.

*Healing from trauma and recovery is acknowledging we have a problem.

*Healing from trauma and recovery is taking positive actions to stop the destructive cycle.

*Healing from trauma and recovery is also about realizing that we are not to blame for the abuse we received as children.

Remember that nothing you could have done warranted the abuse you survived. The abuse I survived was not normal, but in fact extreme and excessive.

Society must come to grips with what John Crewdson wrote in his book 'Silence Betrayed' "the surest way of all to deny a child time and space to discover his capacity for self-love and self-admiration is to abuse him physically, sexually and emotionally." Trauma healing means letting go of the many destructive, fake, isolating Masks we all wear. We *must* do this to break the cycle of abuse.

"NO MORE MASKS = NO MORE SECRETS /

NO MORE SECRETS = NO MORE VICTIMS."

PART ONE

~

"A TIME IN PAIN...

-CHAPTER ONE-

Death of My Inner-Child

My first recollection of being abused by my mother begins
like this: I was three years old and standing on a chair in our hallway.
Mother was trying to measure and pin up the cuffs of a pair of hand-
me-down pants I was wearing that used to belong to my older brother,
Jason, who had just turned six. Mother was growing very impatient.
"Jimmy stand still now. I said stand still. Damn it! Stop moving!
What? The pins hurt. Well, if you would stay still, I'll be done soon.
Now stop fussing around." She said as she swatted me on the butt
'Smack!'

"Now stand up straight and stop whining or I'll give you something
to really cry about. Will you just..." Her patience had run out. Tired
and frustrated, she poked herself with one of the pins and screamed at
me.

"Damn it to hell anyways!" 'Smack!' Mother backhanded me and
knocked me off the chair. I smashed against a bedroom door then
crumpled to the floor. She stood there with her hands on her hips
yelling,

"Now stand up! Come on get up! I haven't got all day. If you'd do
as you're told, I'd be done by now!" I managed to stand up. I was
hurting and frustrated. My hands must have been clinched as I stood

before her, and I was about to learn my first lesson in expressing myself.

She started to come unglued and then she just snapped,

"What's that? Are you making a fist at me James Petra?" She grabbed me by my shirt, picked me up, and stood me back on the chair. She's nose-to-nose with me and I was so frightened. Her every word was seething with anger.

"I'll tell you what little man. I'll give you one free shot." She said her words spraying everywhere like a rabid dog.

"That's right." She continued, "But I swear to God you had better make it count, because when you're through then it'll be my turn you little asshole, and God give you the strength to ever breathe another breath of air again. You had better never and I mean *ever* even think about doubling up your fists at me again. Because, if you do, I guarantee that it will be your last time. I will hurt you so bad; you'll wish you'd never been born. In fact, you're not even supposed to be here. You were supposed to be a girl, you little shit!"

By that time mother was too livid to finish her project.

"Give me them damn pants. I'm through with you today. Get your ass into your room and take a nap." She said with disgust. I cried uncontrollably, as I climbed up into my bed, I felt so sad and confused as I sobbed and gasped for air. I finally managed to calm myself down. I moved my hands down toward my ankles and carefully touched the bleeding pin marks left by mother. Exhausted, finally I drifted off to sleep.

-CHAPTER TWO-

Mother's Weapon of Choice

*H*ot Wheel tracks were the weapon of choice in the Halculm house. One day Jason and I were playing with our Hot Wheel cars and mother came storming into our room screaming at us. In a fit of rage, she picked up one of the orange tracks and started swinging it. She saw that it worked as well as my step-dad's belt, if not a little better. So from then on, our step-dad kept his belts in good shape and mother put Hot Wheel tracks all throughout the house for easy access. She kept one on top of the refrigerator, one tucked between the cushions of the sofa, one on her night stand and we'd play with the rest of them in our room until one of hers wore out then she'd take another one of ours.

It was always a bittersweet experience when one of us boy's received a brand new set of tracks for our birthday. I thought, "Hey, great, new tracks." Then the next day the beatings would begin.

As if having your parents buy you beating sticks on your own birthday wasn't a bummer enough, think how we felt when we saw that all too familiar shaped box laying gift wrapped under the Christmas tree. Even Santa Claus thought we were bad little boys.

One day mother was teaching me how to tie my shoestrings on my shoes, she would say,

"No, do it again!" 'Whack!' As the Hot Wheel track connected across my fingers, tears welled up in my eyes and my little hands trembled. This wasn't helping my attempts to tie the strings correctly.

"No! 'Whack!' Do it again!" Mother said.

I grew up thinking that everyone learned under these conditions. I was just disciplined the most because I was stupid. To me the Hot Wheel track was just an extension of my mother's arm. Unfortunately learning how to make my bed was no different. See footnote at end of this chapter.

When I was four years old, I shared a room with my two brothers. Jason, who was seven, and I had bunk beds; I slept on the bottom bunk. Jack was two and a half and still slept in his crib.

One day mother tried to teach me how to make my bed with hospital corners and all. Mother demonstrated how she wanted the bed to be made.

"Okay, now you make it." She said as she tore the bed apart and handed me the sheets. She left the bedroom. A few minutes later, I was sure I had gotten it just the way she showed me.

"I'm done." I called out. Then when she came to the bedroom door and saw my work, I said, "Like this?" As I looked up at her, I had a slight smile and was in anticipation of her approval.

"Damn it James!" She says, "I wish you'd pay attention and do just one thing right. One thing, that's all I ask!" She huffed as she tore the sheets off the bed again. Then she proceeded to show me how she wanted the job to be completed and told me, "Crease down the middle of the bed. Equal length of sheet on each side and this is how to make a hospital corner at the foot of the bed. See, both sides are nice and tight now." As she tears off the sheets, again she said,

"Do it right this time." Then she left the room.

I can't rightly say how I felt at age four; I can only assume looking back now that a dark gray cloud of sadness started to overtake

Petra / Too Many Masks / Chap. Two

me. Despair reared its ugly head as I started making my bed again.

"Crease down the middle of the bed," I said to myself. However, by then the crease had almost disappeared because of all the making and unmaking of the bed. Trying to make the bottom bunk bed, which is up against the wall, was so difficult anyway because I could not reach the other side without wrinkling up the sheets. I tried to remember word for word exactly what mother told me, and I worked feverishly to accomplish the task.

"Is this exactly half? Is that a triangle?" I asked myself. "How am I supposed to tuck in the other side without messing up what I've already done?" Stepping back to view my work, I knew that I had done my best yet I could see it was not exactly how mother did it. So I waited in silence, sitting on the hardwood floor with my head hung low and anticipating mother's return. I could hear her in the living room folding laundry and watching one of her soap operas. I debated whether to call her in or continue to wait.

"I'm done." I heard myself say hesitantly. Mother entered the room to inspect my work. She reached down and tore off the sheets once again.

"Nope, you do it again." She said sternly as she heaped them into a pile in the middle of the bed. 'Smack!' She hit me across the back of the head.

"Do it right this time or I'll get the hot wheel track out." She said as she huffed out of the room. Eventually she always got out her weapon of choice and came in swinging.

Footnote: The book, 'Adult Children of Abusive Parents', Chapter Eight is entitled, 'Breaking the Cycle' encourages adult children to compliment their own children on even the most smallest of accomplishments. Remember to commend them for even the smallest positive deeds. Perhaps they tried to make their bed but didn't quite do the way you would have. It reminded me of the time mother taught me how to make a bed.

(After I wrote this next experience out on paper, I put it away and read it a few days later. After I read it again, I thought, "My goodness, how could I have remembered all of those details? I was so young when that took place." Then it dawned on me, children are aware of a lot more things than grownups give them credit for. I have read books and I've heard people say, "Younger children won't remember certain experiences when they get older." Well, I am here to tell you, they will remember, even if it does not make any sense in their little minds at the time. Consciously or subconsciously, a traumatic experience, a "little secret" will register in their innocent memory banks and will affect them for the rest of their lives.)

-CHAPTER THREE-

Keeping Secrets

One day when I was four years old, I was walking down the street to visit the Gomez kid's who lived eight houses down from us. They lived on the same side of the street so I did not have to 'look both ways before crossing,' as mother always told us boys. It was a sunny California day and the year was 1968, times were safer in our South Sacramento neighborhood than it is today. My mission included happy plans of playing with cars, little plastic soldiers, Indians, and cowboys in the dirt at my friend's house.

As I got closer to my destination, I noticed that their car was not in the driveway. "No matter," I thought, because back then most people had only one car for the whole family. "Surely someone must be home; and, besides I've come all this way. Oh, I hope they're home. I hope, I hope!" I said to myself. Finally, I reached the house and all was quiet. I was going to ring the doorbell and saw the wires hanging out and remembered it was broken just like the one on our house. So I knocked on the door.

"Come in!" said the voice in the house. Nobody ever locked their door when they were home in those days.

"Come in." I heard once again. So I opened the door and stepped inside. I was happy that my long trek down the block had not been in vain.

"Hi Mr. Gomez." I said while glancing around the room.

"Where is everybody?" I asked.

"Anthony Jr. is at his grandmother's this weekend and Ricky is with his mother and baby sister at the store. They should be home soon. Why not sit and wait for them. They shouldn't be too long!" Mr. Gomez replied.

"Okay." I said as I took a seat on the hardwood floor in the living room. Mother always said, 'Furniture is for grownups and the floor is for little boys who are in the habit of always having dirt on their backsides.' I sat there waiting and playing with one of their toys.

The familiar aroma of corn tortillas and tamales filled the air. Their dinner was on the stove simmering. The Gomez' would have freshly made tortillas with every meal, and hot sauce, always-hot sauce.

"Would you like a flour tortilla with cheese, Jimmy?" Mr. Gomez asked as he walked into the kitchen to check on dinner.

"No thank you." I replied. Mother used to say, 'It's just good manners to decline food when it's offered out of kindness.' Mr. Gomez had finished in the kitchen and returned to the sofa. The steam from the simmering tamales had left droplets on his face. He wiped his forehead with a small towel as he sat down.

"You don't have to sit on the floor. Come over here and sit next to me, I want to show you something." Mr. Gomez told me.

"Okay." I said, and got up quickly and jumped onto the sofa. I knelt next to him, reached up to his face, and wiped a little water off the man's cheek.

"Thank you." Mr. Gomez said smiling. "You are such a nice young man, James." He continued to say nice things that made me feel good and special. Then I sat next to him and waited politely for what he was going to show me. Mr. Gomez kept glancing out the living room window as if he were watching for someone.

"I want to show you something and it will be our little secret." He said.

I knew about secrets because my big brother Jason and I would keep secrets from our little brother.

"Okay!" I exclaimed. I treasured any positive attention because, in the Halculm household, anything positive was scarce. Mr. Gomez looked out the window and then back at me.

"Look at this!" He said, as he unzipped his pants and pulled out his Tallywacker. Tallywacker was what my mother called a penis. He sat there rubbing himself. Then he reached over, unzipped my shorts, and started fondling my little penis. Mr. Gomez then bent over, kissed my belly, and then went lower. I was surprised to be sure, but I said nothing. I just sat there. My little friend's dad sat back on the sofa and asked me to kiss his penis. Well, it was the biggest one I had ever seen. I had never seen a grownup's Tallywacker before. I had only seen my two brothers. Why, I just sat there and marveled at the large hairy thing.

"Go ahead, it's okay. Kiss it." Said Mr. Gomez. So obediently (1) - - see footnote, I bent across his lap and kissed it. He sat there rubbing himself and pointed his penis toward me as I laid there with just my shorts on, which were still down below my knees. Suddenly something squirted out of this man's large penis and landed on my belly and down my little thigh. I was amazed and struck with wonder because it certainly was not pee. This was different and sticky too.

"Here" Mr. Gomez said, "Let me clean it off you." As he took the kitchen towel, he had and wiped my belly off. All of the sudden a car pulled up into the driveway.

"Quick, Maria and the kids are home!" Mr. Gomez stammered as he hurriedly pulled up his pants and tugged up my shorts.

"Now, this is our little secret, okay?" He said to me, as he gave me a nice pat on the head.

I went outside to greet my friends and ran off to play in their backyard. I put that curious ordeal behind me, not knowing that similar episodes would happen through the next year and a half.

The special attention made me feel good, I was good at keeping secrets, I just didn't like the taste of Mr. Gomez' penis when I was told to suck on it. It was big and I almost choked a time or two.

The last time an incident happened was when Mr. Gomez and his wife came over to our house, one evening to play cards with my parents. Jason and I were in our bedroom playing when I heard those same words again.

"Come here Jimmy." Mr. Gomez said as he poked his head out the bathroom door. I was miffed because he was interrupting my playing. Obediently I went into our small bathroom and closed the door. He had his penis out and was playing with it, as he said,

"Here kiss it. Don't you want to kiss it?" He asked. I remember just looking at it, in disgust and I said,

"No. No I don't. I don't want to kiss it anymore." Then, without waiting for a reply, I darted out the door and went back to my bedroom where Jason was still playing.

"What did he want?" Jason asked me.

"Oh, nothing." I huffed, but he persisted.

"Tell me, what did he want?"

"He, he... wanted to show me something on his shirt. He had a spot on it. I don't know, he didn't know what it was and I didn't either." I said as I shrugged my shoulders and resumed playing. Jason quirked his head and pondered a little, then he too went back to playing.

That abusive relationship ended that night between Mr. Gomez and I. His secret remained safe with me. Of all the things mother taught us about safety and being polite, she never told us about personal boundaries or limits of touching. Looking back now, of course, she lacked certain boundaries herself.

"Compliance is not the same as consent."

Footnote (1) I learned something so very important in my Trauma healing. It's an affirmation that should be remembered by anybody who is in any kind of relationship, but especially those who abuse children. "Compliance is not the same as consent." Any child who is seventeen years old and under, cannot give consent or permission, no matter how willing they are, they are the child and you are the adult. (U.S.A.) Children have a need to please or be obedient for acceptance. Sadly, some adults and older kids take advantage of that knowledge.

-CHAPTER FOUR-

Rude Awakening (1) – see footnote

Like most parents, there were times when mother and our step-dad, Rodger, went out for the evening and left us with a babysitter. Of course, we had to be on our very best behavior during the evening or it would mean death. We were *never* any trouble for them. We had chores of one kind or another to do. If we forgot or did not do it just right, then we were in for a rude awakening from mother when they got home.

They usually came home anywhere between 11:00 pm to 2:00 am. While Rodger took the sitter home, mother came storming into our bedroom, threw open the door, turn on the lights then 'Smack!' she would hit us anywhere that was conveniently exposed. Whomever it was that did not do a particular job just exactly the way she had instructed was the target. She would grab us from our beds and throw us towards the door. Maybe a serving spoon was not put in the correct area of the drawer, or a Tupperware lid was mixed in with the lids for the pots and pans. One time there was water left standing behind the kitchen faucet. Another time, the kitchen trashcan was not pulled out and swept behind. Any such mistakes merited punishment.

Jason and I always tried so hard to make sure that everything was done just right. She didn't always find something wrong, but she did it enough times for us to see a pattern. Most of the time I would try to keep awake until they got home, just in case mother found a reason to wake us and beat the crap out of us. It didn't matter which one of us got beat, we were both scared to death for ourselves and for each other.

The next day I was always exhausted from staying up late listening to mother's footsteps as she made her way through the house checking things out. I couldn't relax until I knew she was in bed. It usually took me awhile to calm down enough to fall asleep. Morning always came too soon; I often had trouble staying awake in school. My teacher would ask me why I was so sleepy. I always lied to her and said that I stayed up late watching television. By the time I got home from school, mother found out about my lie and was ready to beat me again for lying. These beatings were followed by the never-ending supply of bar soap that mother kept for cursors and liars to eat.

~

While I am still on the subject of rude awakenings and "the things I hated when mother did..." She had this routine of waking up her children:

Every morning was the same. She threw open our bedroom door as it smashed against the wall. (Rodger never bothered to fix the hole where the doorknob had broken through the sheetrock. It seemed pointless.) Mother turned on the light, and immediately started pounding on the hollow core door with both her fists, and began yelling,

"Up and at em, rise, and shine, let's go, let's go. Rise and shine!" 'Bang, bang, rattle, bang!' She didn't stop until we were all out of bed and standing on the floor.

"We're up, we're up!" We would say, just hoping she would stop the racket. Each and every day, this was how our little bodies were jolted out of our beds.

~

While we're on the topic of doors, if we left a door open, or if we came through in a hurry and a door slammed shut, usually it was the garage door, which was solid wood, mother took our fingers, placed them in the door jam and slam the door on them. Even if it wasn't our fault, like when the wind would catch it, it didn't matter. Whoever went through the door last got their fingers slammed in the door. She did it several times until the skin on our knuckles pealed, she literally looked at our fingers, and she only stopped when she saw blood. Garage doors are not the hollow core doors like the interior bedroom doors; they're thicker, heavier, and stronger doors. Sometimes she even put our head in the door jam and slammed the door as hard as she could, two maybe three times. She said that she wanted to 'get it through our thick skull,' how to properly open and close a door.

Footnote (1) the book "Adult children of Abusive parents" has a writing exercise: "Make a list of 10 things;" starting with a sentence, "I hate it when Dad did this, or that. I hate it when Mother did this, or that." The exercise helped me to remember these next experiences in this chapter.

-CHAPTER FIVE-

Table Manners

*W*hen we put our elbows on the table during a meal, mother invariably poked our arms with her fork. How many times and how hard she poked depended on her mood, sometimes she drew blood.

Once when I was six, I recall getting in trouble for not eating properly. Mother got so incensed that she spat as she declared,

"You eat like a damn animal! If you like to eat like an animal, then you go eat on the floor with the animals!" She made me eat on the floor. I was told to put my plate on the floor. I had to keep my hands at my side as I ate the rest of my dinner with only my mouth. However, that still wasn't good enough for mother. She actually called out for one of our cats to come into the kitchen.

"Here kitty, kitty, kitty." She called out as she put some dry cat food on my plate. So I not only had mashed potatoes all over my face with gravy and green beans everywhere, but now I was sharing my plate with an animal. I was so humiliated. I began to cry. However, what worried me most was that I had my back to her. I was more afraid about not being able to see when she was going to hit me. I had no ability to brace myself or flinch and I was utterly terrified. This combined with the sheer degradation of being laughed at by the whole family. The fact that I was treated like, and made to feel dumber than an animal, seemed to do the trick for her that night. Even the cat sensed the tension in the air and after a few bites, the situation got too weird even for him to stick around, so he left. Oh how I wished I could have left too.

I was crying and shaking, as I tried to hurry up and get that nightmare over with, I accidentally ate some of the cat food that was mixed together with my own dinner.

"Don't eat the damn cat food you idiot!" Mother yelled, then 'Pow!' She swiftly kicked me in my side and I toppled over and hit the kitchen cabinet. What was left of the food on my plate was overturned and slid into the corner.

Finally, the dinner entertainment was over.

"Clean yourself and this mess up. Then get your ass to bed. Next time you'll think twice about your table manners and how young gentlemen are supposed to eat." Mother said.

I remember having to go through the same hell another time that same year. I don't remember what I was doing wrong. I could have been eating too fast, or smacking my food, or maybe I was talking with my mouth full. Any one of those things made mother go berserk.

To this day, when I see people in some eating contest where they can't use their hands and they have food smeared all over their faces, I just cringe and flashback to that night. Sometimes, when I'm watching with a friend they'll ask me,

"Hey Jimbo, doesn't that look fun?"

"Yeah, Real fun." I'd sarcastically reply.

~

Later that same year, I had bed-wetting accidents. Mother punished me by putting a diaper on me and made me play outside in the front yard. We lived in front of my elementary school. When I tried to hide by our porch, mother drug me out by the sidewalk. Words cannot describe how utterly humiliated I was, six years old, sitting there in the grass with nothing on but a cloth diaper. I hung my head and wished I was somewhere else. I'd think to myself, "I'm not here, this is not happening. Please let me disappear." As my friends laughed at me as they walked by.

-CHAPTER SIX-

Two Helpings of Thanksgiving Dinner

It was 1971, Thanksgiving Day, at the Halculm house. My brothers and I woke up to the smells of holiday preparations. Mother was already in the kitchen getting the bird ready for the oven. We knew it was not going to be a day of leisure. There were chores to be done from a list that mother kept in her head. So after a quick breakfast of cold cereal and English muffins, it was full speed ahead.

Mother and Rodger had invited their friends, Allen and Pauline Westercott, over to share in the festivities. Allen worked with my step dad. He and Pauline came over to play cards and visit from time to time. We were all looking forward to having a great time that day.

I wasn't feeling very well when I got up that morning, but not bad enough to complain about it. So Jason and I, along with our little brother Jack, filed into the kitchen, quickly ate our meal, and were soon into cleaning the house. Before we knew it, everything was completed and our guests had arrived.

The Westercotts did not have any children at the time. The adults sat at the dining table, my brothers and I sat at the kid's table, which my step-dad had set up beside the refrigerator. I was still not feeling much better, but I didn't want to bother mother with my problems. (How many six-year-old children do you know that are afraid to tell their mother that they're sick?) She was very busy with the day's activities. So I sat and ate my full plate of all the traditional goodies: turkey, mashed potatoes and gravy, yams with those little marshmallows, cranberry sauce, rolls, and stuffing. The closer I was to finishing the food on my plate, the slower I ate. My tummy started to gurgle and rumble. Little beads of sweat formed on my brow. I had finished my last bite of dinner on my plate, then in a flash my dinner came right back up. There was no time to rush to the bathroom and no time to move. Vomit came out and landed on my plate, filling it to the top edge.

The room fell silent. All eyes turned towards the disgusting sound and the pungent smell that soon enveloped the room. I just froze, my eyes quickly filled with tears. I glanced over to mother who looked at me with great anger and rage. The look on her face seemed to say, "I worked so hard on this meal and this is the thanks you give me? How dare you!" I don't recall her getting up; I only remember her smacking me on the back of the head as hard as she could. Then mother sternly told me,

"You will sit there and eat every last drop of that before you're dismissed from this table."

So there I was, sobbing uncontrollably. I picked up my fork, but with my little hands shaking, I dropped it. 'Smack!' came another slap on the top of my already throbbing head. I could not believe what mother was making me do. But, I knew all too well that even thinking of talking back to her would mean certain death. So I picked up my spoon. My head was spinning with pain and my tummy was pitted with nervous quivers. I scooped up a spoonful of my vomit and placed it in my mouth. The awful taste was still in my mouth and throat from when it came up moments earlier, but it was the smell I had to fight through and the fear that any moment I might throw up again.

Mother took away my glass of water. I don't know how I managed, but I finally finished my plate while everyone else went to the living room to watch the Thanksgiving Day Parade on the television. Jason and mother were cleaning up the kitchen and getting ready to serve pumpkin pie. Needless to say, I didn't want my piece. I was finally excused from the table and I went to my room and cried myself to sleep.

~

Reflecting back on the experience I often ask myself, "What did the Westercotts think about what happened that day?" I don't remember how they reacted on that particular day, but I do know that no one ever stepped in between mother and her wrath. I guess, maybe, she rarely showed her violent rage in front of company.

Allen and Pauline used to baby-sit us every once and a while. We stayed at their house most of those time. Trying to be the little gentlemen that we were trained to be, we asked if there were any chores around their house that we could do. Pauline always made our small gesture of kindness into a big production for us.

"Well thank you so much for helping with the lunch dishes. You are such big helpers, and you worked so hard on them. I am so proud of you." She said that as she knelt down and gave me the biggest hug I'd ever had. She almost squeezed the life out of me but I didn't mind because I loved every minute of it. I didn't even bother to wipe off the icky kiss she gave me on my cheek.

"I think I'll just brag all over you when your folks come to pick you guys up." She said boastfully. We all smiled from ear to ear and danced around the room with glee. Little did Pauline know that her words of praise would eventually come back to bite us. You see mother never understood why children always performed better at other peoples home and were more willing to clean up someone else's room then to do their own at home. This infuriated her to no end and the beatings intensified.

"Why don't you mind and do as you're told when I tell you to do something here at home?" She screamed into my face as she tried to shake some sense into me, she continued mockingly,

"You're such a *big helper* and you work *so hard...*" She then made me stand at attention in front of her as she sat on the couch with the hot wheel track in hand. My shirt off and my back was towards her. She calmly and sternly asked me,

"Why don't you mind me?"

"I don't know." I replied, as I stood there crying and shaking with fear. Then I braced myself the best I could for the beating to begin, realizing that my answer was not what she wanted to hear. 'WHACK.'

"Nope, wrong answer. Why do I have to repeat myself so many times before you do what you're told?" She yelled above my cries of pain.

"I don't know." I said again. Then, 'WHACK.'

"Nope, wrong again..." 'WHACK'...

This went on for what seemed like hours and until her arms got tired of swinging the track. I never was able to think of a different reply. Finally, she made me finish whatever chore I was supposed to do in the first place. After which she usually made me go to bed without dinner, which was fine with me because I was always exhausted from going through such a hopeless and painful ordeal.

Throughout the years, Allen and Pauline continued to babysit us kids from time to time. Each time we offered to help, and each time sweet Pauline commended us on a job well done. I always said thank you but I'm sure it lacked conviction.

"It's no big deal." I'd tell her shrugging my shoulders as I looked towards the ground. She seemed to sense the unspoken meaning behind my response and perhaps felt the powerlessness of the situation too. She still always offered a kind word and a big hug whenever she could.

~

Recently I was at a used bookstore that also sold old vinyl records. I found one that I remembered was one of mother's favorites. I don't recall what possessed me to purchase it but I did. I took it home and played it and as soon as I heard the music and words to the songs, I instantly felt calm. After a few songs played, I stopped the record and wondered why those songs had such a calming effect on me. Then it dawned on me, mother played her vinyl records when she cleaned house. She took care not to scratch them, meaning when she got mad at us she walked over to the record player and took the needle off the record and secured it. Then the beatings began. So for me, when I heard the music it meant I was safe. When the music stopped, all hell broke loose. You know like when people are playing Musical Chairs, I never did like to play or watch it, because when the music stops in mid song and everybody reacts to it, I picture myself scrambling for safety, or bracing myself, waiting to be hit.

This reminded me of other times I felt safe too, like when we went to the Sacramento Zoo or across the street to William Land Park. I remember the day I had a revelation, it dawned on me at six years old that mother was somebody else when we were in a crowd. We were allowed to play, run, climb, laugh, and have a good time when people were present. I felt safe, people were smiling, and smiles are safe. It meant as long as I saw smiles, nobody was getting beat.

-CHAPTER SEVEN-

Mother's Day Present

*I*t was springtime and a week before Mother's Day. My first grade teacher wanted our class to do an art project for Mother's Day. At the start of that project, someone in class suggested,

"Let's make this a surprise Mother's Day gift."

"Okay, yeah, this will be great!" Said another student. So all week long, we toiled and had a splendid time. Everyone in class was going to make nice big daffodils. We took yellow construction paper and cut out the petals. Then, from a single section of an egg flat, we cut and painted yellow for the trumpet shaped center. We cut out a stem and two leaves from a piece of green construction paper. We arranged all the pieces on a sky blue piece of paper. We had each made a bright, beautiful, hand created 'Springtime Daffodil.' It was made with all the love and pride that a six-year-old child could have for his mom.

I was so proud of my flower. It had taken me the whole week of art time to make it.

On the Friday, just before Mother's Day, Jason and I got up and made our own breakfast. We did so quietly, because mother went back to sleep after waking us up. Hurrying around the house to get off to school on time, everything was going routinely until, being the klutz that I was, I bumped the end table. I successfully caught the lamp, but I wasn't able to grab the small, single stem, flower vase. 'SMASH!' went the sound of mother's vase as it hit the floor. Both Jason and I stood silently for what seemed like an eternity. We were horrified at breaking something, but even more terrified at the possibility of waking up mother. You *never* made noise in the morning, because, if mother had to get up to see what all the commotion was about, she was going to make it worth her while and heads were going to roll.

Staring at each other, Jason and I stood very still, barely breathing and listening for any sounds coming from mother's room...we heard nothing... we were safe. I carefully picked up the shattered vase and put the pieces in the trashcan in the kitchen. Jason and I agreed that it would be better to tell mother about the accident after we got home from school. So we scurried out the door and walked to school.

The day went by fast, after school, I went over to the art table and picked up my beautiful yellow daffodil for mother. I felt so proud and excited about surprising mother with a masterpiece that was worthy of being posted on the refrigerator art gallery.

I just couldn't get home fast enough. I ran home and barely made it to the front porch steps without falling. I was fumbling with my books and lunch box, trying not to crinkle mother's surprise. I finally reached the doorknob when the door flew open. Mother was there to greet me. My little face radiated a smile, which quickly vanished as mother grabbed me by the arm, yanked me into the house, and slammed the door. Mother yelled,

"What in Sam Hell happened to my antique vase?" She snapped,

"How did you break it?"

Jason had gotten home shortly before me and she had already interrogated him. She grabbed a hold of me by my shoulders and screamed,

"Do you realize that, that vase was a wedding gift from your grandmother? It was a family heirloom! When you broke it, why didn't you tell me about it this morning? Why did I have to find it in the trashcan, you Son of a Bitchin' Kid?" All the while, she's shaking me so hard that I drop everything all over the living room. 'SMACK!' went mother's hand across my face. 'SMACK!' again. That time she connected with my ear, so from then on, as she continued shouting at me, the ringing in my head muffled the sound of her voice. Shaken and crying I apologized profusely about the accident.

"I'm sorry!" I said, "I'm so sorry!" Standing there trembling. I thought to myself, "I didn't know the vase meant so much to her. I knew I would be in some kind of trouble for breaking it, but I didn't know it was from grandma."

After a while, mother calmed down a little. She picked up my lunch box and I picked up my books and my art project.

"What's that?" Mother huffed. I told her, with tears still in my eyes and a quiver in my voice,

"It's your Mother's Day present. I made it at school." I showed it to her, hoping it would help smooth things over.

"It is, huh?" She said as she took it from me. "Well, this is what I think of it!" Then she ripped it into shreds and said, "There, see. You ruin something of mine; I'll ruin something of yours. I bet you worked hard on it too. Well, you just remember this the next time you break something that isn't yours. You understand me?" Then she threw the flower into the trash and said, "Now, you get your ass in your room and you sit on that floor. You are grounded for the weekend. Get out of my sight." I went to my room very saddened. I felt bad because I had broken mother's vase, and *really* sad over the fact that I had worked so hard all week to make a present for mother that I was so proud of, and proud to give it to my mother whom I loved so very much. Then to watch her tear it up without even glancing at it before she threw it in the trash like something worthless it was devastating.

She did it with not even an inkling of a care. I look back now and realize that what my mother did that day hurt and cut deep into my very soul. I was filled with sadness. From that day forward, it was like a dark storm cloud followed me around for a very long time, getting bigger and darker as the years dragged on.

-CHAPTER EIGHT-

Just a Dream

One night while sleeping, I had a dream. It was so real, I woke up and was startled. I thought I was late for school. I sat up in my bed and exclaimed,

"Mom, Mom, I'm late. I'm late!" I said in a daze. Mother had just opened the bedroom door to check on us kids before retiring for the night. I didn't realize it was only 10:20 pm.

"For what?" She asked.

"I'm late for school!" I anxiously told her.

"Well then, you'd better hurry and get up. You mustn't be late!" She said. Rodger was returning from making sure the house was closed up and everything secured for the evening.

"What's going on?" He asked, and mother proceeded to fill him in on what was happening and without missing a beat, he too was in on the fun.

"Well, hurry. Yes hurry, we mustn't be late. Come on, get up, and get dressed." Rodger chimed in.

They both helped me find everything to wear. While I was dressing, I woke up enough to know that something was amiss. I was the only child getting up for school.

"Come now, you don't want to be late!" One of them said as they both ushered me into the living room.

"Now sit right there on the sofa and wait until it's time to go to school. Don't you dare go to sleep, or you'll be in big trouble if you miss going to school on time." Mother said.

By the time I sat on the sofa, I was pretty much awake and just sitting there so confused. I wondered how I got myself into this predicament. My parents had left and turned off all the lights and went to bed. So there I sat and did not dare fall asleep. There was nothing more terrifying than being in a sound sleep and then being awakened by mother's powerful slap and being thrown by the force of her opened hand as it connected across your face.

It was a very long night. I could hear the cars driving by our house. The faint beam of light from the street pole peeked in through the drapes and kept me company as the night dragged on. I sat up as straight as I could and fought back Mr. Sandman with all of my might. Just when I thought he was winning, I caught a second wind and sat up straight again. This went on for seven hours, until I heard Rodgers alarm clock go off in my parent's room.

My step-dad finally made it up and walked through the living room to the kitchen to start the percolator for his morning coffee. He looked down at me in disbelief and asked,

"Have you been up all night?" I was confused by his question because he was right there when mother told me not to fall asleep or I'd be in big trouble.

"Yes sir." I replied. He just shook his head and went on his merry way. He left for work shortly after that without saying another word. Silence filled the house once again for another hour. By then the sun was peeking through the drapes anywhere it could, as if it was going to burst them open at any moment. Mother finally woke up and started her daily routine. At least I wasn't jolted awake by her banging on our bedroom door, like my brothers were. I could hear Jason saying through the racket,

"Okay, we're up, we're up!" Little Jack was crying in the background. I was finally able to get up from the sofa and go to the bathroom. Then I ate breakfast with Jason and went to school. Needless to say, I was extremely tired as the day dragged on. My first grade teacher asked me again why I was so sleepy. I made up an excuse and once again, I returned home to get beat for lying. Once again, she made me eat another bar of soap.

-CHAPTER NINE-

"An Old Expression Becomes a Reality"

To most people it's just a figure of speech; but for me, the saying 'Getting the crap beat out of you', really happened to me. This took place the Halloween of 1972. I was seven years old at the time and I don't recall what I had done wrong to be grounded from 'Trick or Treating' with my brothers. I was so very sad about this because I wasn't going to get my pillowcase full of candy too.

Unfortunately, missing out on trick or treating that evening wasn't good enough for mother. Oh no, she also made me stand at the door and pass out candy. She didn't even let me wear my costume. I was so humiliated when kids from school came by and saw me.

"Hey, Jimmy," They said, "Why aren't you out here 'Trick or Treating' and where's your costume?" There was nowhere to hide and I couldn't lie because mother was standing behind the door. So looking down, I mumbled,

"I was a bad boy this year."

"Oh," They replied, "Well, see ya at school then." I wished the kids would stop coming up to our house, but to no avail. I had to open the door again and again to happy schoolmate's greetings,

"Trick or Treat, hey Jimmy, where's your costume?" They would ask.

"I don't get to wear it because I was bad." Mother told me what to say and add, "I was a bad little boy this year." The humiliation continued. If she did not think I said it loud enough the first time, she made me repeat it. After an hour or so of that, she realized that my plight was making some of the kids feel sorry for me, so she started passing out the candy and then shooing the kids away. She made sure the humiliation factor was still present because I had to stand there so my friends could still see me.

All my friends brought tons of candy to school throughout the week. They had candy in their lunch boxes and candy in their pockets, sharing with those who had some to trade. The humiliation I felt Halloween night lasted through the rest of the week.

"Jimmy, where's your candy?" My friends asked. The ones who didn't know my plight already asked,

"What did you dress up as for Halloween?" The other kids who knew were jeering and mocking me by replying,

"Poor little Jimmy was a bad boy this year and he wasn't allowed to go get any candy." I was very, very sad. Then I started to get mad at them and angry with my mother. I started to crave candy. The smell of it filled the air all week long. "I love candy, too!" I said to myself.

One day during recess, I was visiting with my friend Tony, who was quite chubby. I told him I was so jealous of everyone else having Halloween candy.

"Why don't we go to the store and get us some." He said, though I didn't know why because neither one of us had any money.

"When I'm with my mom at the store, sometimes I steal a little candy when nobody is looking." This intrigued me. We talked some more and we agreed to meet the next day at lunch. The next day we ran to the nearest market to try out our little plan to steal some candy.

My heart was pounding from running and from the fear of

getting caught. We did it. We stole some candy and made it out of the store without being caught. Now we had to run back to school before anybody noticed we were gone. I thought to myself, "Wow, what a success! What a rush! I had candy, my very own candy." I devoured every morsel greedily. I felt like I was on top of the world.

We did it again two more times that week. Each time I felt my heart in my throat. I was so afraid of being caught because I knew it would mean death for me. "This will be the last time!" I told myself every time we did it. Soon the candy was gone. The candy did not seem to taste as good as it did, when we first stole it from the market. Guilt and worry were my constant companions.

One day our luck finally ran out. A cashier woman had noticed us repeatedly coming into the store and leaving without buying anything. She caught us red handed and brought us up to the front of the store where we emptied out our pockets. I begged her not to call my mother and that we would never do it again we were so scared and crying. We put the goods on the counter and split out of the store. We ran faster than we ever had before.

"Maybe we'll get back before she calls the school and we'll just blend in and tell them we've been there all along." Tony said as we ran. But, no such luck for us. Our teacher caught us coming into the school ground and reprimanded us. I hoped that she wouldn't call my mother. I thought, "Maybe she'll forget to call. Maybe she'll see that we put the candy back so there's no harm done." Again, no such luck. Mother was at the front door to greet me when I got home after school. She seemed to enjoy doing that, warning us of impending doom.

"You are so dead." She told me, "Just you wait until daddy gets home. Until then, stay in your room. Sit on the floor, no playing, and no dinner. We don't feed little thieves in this house. You just sit there and think about what you've done and what's going to happen to you tonight."

Later on, that night I noticed the curtains were pulled closed in the living room. My brothers were getting ready for bed. The evening had ended for everyone but me. I had been sitting in my room waiting since I got home from school. Waiting and fretting as a little seven year old would.

I imagined that the punishment that night would merit a long beating with a thick, industrial sized, yellow Hot Wheel track. Mother said she was not in the mood for chasing the kid all around the living room, after each blow. So she had me lay on the floor in front of the sofa where she was sitting. She made me get completely naked and lay face down on the carpet. Then she had my step-dad place the coffee table over half of my body, pinning my head and arms down between the two rod-iron legs at one end. I heard Rodger yell,

"Let the beatings begin!" Mother began. 'Whack, Whack, Whack!' across my bare butt and squirming little legs. All the while, my screams and pleadings went unanswered. 'Whack, Whack, Whack!'

"Ouch, please stop. Okay, I'll be good. I won't do it again!" I vowed these promises in vain. 'Whack, Whack, Whack!' My step-dad had to sit on top of the coffee table because I was moving around too much. Mother was still sitting on the sofa not missing a blow. 'Whack, Whack, Whack!' Blow after blow. Mother had to change hands from time to time, I guess because her arms were getting tired. 'Whack, Whack, Whack!'

"Here Daddy, you want to put in a couple hits?" Mother asked, over the sound of my blood curdling screams.

"Sure, why not." He replied. So while he was still perched on top of the table, he also beat me with the track, 'Whack, Whack, Whack!'

"Here you go. Thanks." He said as he returned the weapon back to mother. By that time, I was in utter despair. The beating would not stop. I was pinned down with nowhere to run for relief. Blow after blow and scream after scream, I didn't have the strength to tighten up and try to prepare for the blows. 'Whack, Whack, Whack!' Finally, felling utterly helpless and at the end of my rope, I screamed with all the energy I had left,

"Help me, please, somebody please help me!"

I thought they were going to kill me, and it was at that point that the timeless expression came to life for me. They had indeed literally beaten the crap out of me. 'Whack, Whack, Whack!'...

"Oh, for crying out loud, look at what blockhead did" Mother said to my step-dad. "Damn it to hell anyways." She continued. "Alright, let him up so he can clean himself off. Come on get up. Poor baby shit himself." She mocked. Still crying I got up trying to catch my breath my mouth was so dry and my tears so thick I could barely see. I staggered into the bathroom trembling. My little legs could barely support me. Blood was trickling down my legs. It hurt to sit down on the toilet. Though shaking and crying, I managed to clean myself off.

"Come on, hurry up!" Mother yelled. "We're not through yet." I obeyed, but was still begging for mercy as I entered the living room. Mother was still wiping the crap off the yellow Hot Wheel track; I could tell that she was still filled with hatred.

"You poor little baby, you shit yourself. Do baby want a diaper?" She sneered. In spite of my pleadings, the beatings continued as I resumed the position on the floor. The coffee table was returned, pinning me my naked body down again. I laid there face down, completely exhausted and defeated. My will to live had left me. I barely recall being hit again, 'Whack, Whack!' then nothing. The whole world went dark. I don't remember anything nothing after that. Apparently, my survivor's skills had failed me. My will to live and my fight to stay alive left me. I blacked out. I couldn't remember the rest of the ordeal. I only recall that over the next few days, mother, my brothers, and I went to visit family in Washington State. It wasn't until I was an adult that my aunt Rhonda asked me if I knew why my mother made those sudden trips to Washington during the school year. I told her no. She said it was because I needed some time to heal up from mother's beatings. I had no idea, and from ages four through eleven years old, I was too young to put it all together. I always remembered the fun we had traveling up to Washington in a Greyhound bus to visit our relatives.

Our visits usually lasted a week or two. I guess it depended on how long it took my wounds to heal. My real father lived a short distance from mother's relatives. On each trip just before returning to California, mother called up my father and step-mom and invited them to come visit Jason and I before we left for the bus depot. I remembered the quick hellos and hugs. I never realized that everything was so well planned and meticulously thought out by Mother. She had a reply, or should I say a lie, for every question.

What a shock to find out that her own family knew why she made those trips. As far as I knew, they did nothing to stop or try to help us boys from "the abuse," as my aunt rightly called it. After I found out, I just figured: "Well, if my family knew about it and no one took action, then I must have deserved the discipline; it just wasn't a big deal. Hey, I lived through it, I must be okay then, right?" I guess that is what dysfunctional families are all about.

My abuse was tragically ignored. Although I do remember when I was in the first and second grades, on occasion I was called to the nurse's office and told to lift up my shirt or my pant legs. I do not recall too much of what was asked or what my replies were. What on earth were my teachers and school nurse waiting for? How much proof did they need prove that I was being abused? Were they so gullible to believe my stories?

"Jason and I were just roughhousing around, it was an accident." And or, I'd say. "We were fighting with each other and he did that to me."

Was I that good of a liar? That abuse had been a tragic, caustic Secret, until now.

~

I also remember after this particular beating took place, mother had us go to the bathroom before she started beating us. This proved only to heighten our stress level to the impending doom. Through those years I remember the pain of my healing wounds, I had trouble walking, in part because of the beatings themselves, but also because the blood and scabs would stick to my clothing. When I needed to use the restroom at school, I cried to myself in the restroom stall because when I pulled down my underwear the wounds reopened and they hurt all over again. Just being beat the next day or two, back to back, hurt worse because the wounds had no time to heal.

I remember the beatings in the wintertime she aimed and hit us on the butt and legs more because we wore pants to school to cover the welts, bruises, and blood. Arms where far game too because she had us wear long sleeve shirts. During the summer time though, she had us stand with our hands on our head, this allowed her to beat us without hitting our arms. She aimed mostly at our butts and backs, because we wore shorts outside.

To this day, the smell of bleach disturbs me because my mother used a lot of bleach to clean the bloodstains off our bed sheets, pillowcases and under clothes.

~

Jason and I spent so much time grounded in our room. We had to sit on the hardwood floor from the time we ate breakfast until the time we went to bed that night. We were only allowed to get off the floor to eat or to quickly use the bathroom. We couldn't play with our toys. We were not allowed to talk but sometimes we did when we knew mother was at the other end of the house or when she went outside, even then we would whisper if we dared say anything at all. We just had to set there; sometimes Jason counted all of the little nails that were in our bedroom floor. It gave us something to do to pass the time.

When my brother Jason was "disciplined" for something, I could hear mother screaming at him and the sound of the hot wheel track connecting to his body, followed by his cries and pleadings. I flinched every time I heard the 'Whack!' Oh how I wished for mother to stop. I felt so utterly powerless, having to hear my big brother go through that hell. Sometimes I wished it were me instead of him, I cried right along with Jason in the other room.

I knew he felt the same way towards me because when it was me getting beat, I would go back to our bedroom afterwards and he too would be crying. We would hug each other then he'd sneak into the bathroom for a cold washcloth to put on the bleeding welts. He was my hero during our childhood years.

We weren't always grounded to the floor in our room. Sometimes mother had us stand in the corner with our noses touching the corner of the wall, which made it very hard to breathe. Sometimes it would last all weekend or sometimes an entire week after we got home from school until bedtime.

My recent research has helped me to understand why society let me down when I needed them the most. The book 'Adult Children of Abusive Parents' states that the first modern child abuse reporting law was not passed until 1964, the same year I was born. Like most new things, it took time to catch on. The book, 'A Fine Line- When

Discipline Becomes Child Abuse,' explains, "President Ford signed public law 93-247 child abuse prevention and treatment act in 1974. By 1977 most states had responded with regulations and required reporting and protecting child services investigations."

When I was in my twenties, I ran into one of our old next-door neighbors. The conversation went something like this.

"My, it's so good to see you and now you're all grown up. I can still remember when you kids were little. Wilbur and I used to sit at our kitchen table and listen to your mother yelling at you little guys then we heard you boys screaming and crying. We often had to close our window... my, it's just so nice to see you today." I just smiled as she told me her story. Once again, I thought to myself, even as an adult, "Well, it must not have been too big of a deal if they knew about it and did nothing to stop it. We must have deserved being disciplined that way." I even felt embarrassed and apologized for disturbing their meals. Even then, I felt I had to stuff my feelings, the hurt and the pain. I had to nullify and dismiss them.

-CHAPTER TEN-

Water Logged

Later that same year, mother was furious with me again about something I had done. Mother and I were in the kitchen. I was too small to reach the sink without standing on a chair, so mother was yelling at me to fetch one, while she turned on the water. As I positioned the chair, she was carrying on saying that nothing she ever said sank into my thick head. So she was going to soak it for a while, then maybe, that would help get it through to me.

She turned on the faucet and it wasn't the cold side. She placed her hand under the running water until it got too hot for her to keep it there. As I stood on the chair, I was completely horrified.

"Please don't mommy. Please, please don't. I'll be good. I'll remember, please don't." I was begging and crying, as she took my T-shirt off so it wouldn't get wet. I was staring down in the sink as the steam bellowed forth from the scalding hot water. Mother took me by the back of the neck and forced my head under the scalding hot water, for ten, fifteen, twenty seconds, and then she raised my head up. I gasped for air, but it was hard to cry and breathe at the same time. She dunked me again, and again. I gulped in water and air. I couldn't understand a word mother was screaming at me. I was too busy begging,

"Please, mommy. Mommy it hurts, please stop!" However, she wasn't listening. She just pushed me under again one more time. The pain was so unbearable and I was so frightened. I thought to myself, "Is she trying to drown me?" Just when I thought I couldn't hold my breath any longer, she pulled my head up. I desperately gasped for air. At that moment, my legs collapsed from under me. Then mother stood me up on the chair again. She was still out of control. She kept dunking me until the water was too hot for her to bear.

Finally, mother lifted me up like a wet rag doll and put me on the floor. She handed me a towel and sent me to my room. I thought to myself, "It's over. I'm still alive. I can't believe it, it's over!" But, it wasn't over yet. It happened again the next evening. By the third night, I had lost all sense of time. How long was I under the scalding water? I did not care. Would I live through another night of hell? I didn't know, nor did I even care. I had no more strength and no more will. With my hands at my side, as I was told, the piping hot water ran down my neck, down my back and burned down my little legs. It happened eight, nine and ten times, until mother got tired. Then she threw me to the ground and I crashed against the refrigerator.

"Get up!" She snapped. "Get up and get out of here. I don't want to see you again this evening." She spat in disgust. Not moving fast enough for her, she grabbed the Hot Wheel track that fell off the top of the fridge when I'd hit it earlier. Then she whipped my scalded little legs 'Whack, Whack, Whack!' She connected every time.

I scrambled to my feet and ran through the house. I missed tripping over the coffee table only by an inch. I couldn't believe I made it to my room where I found my bed, a safe haven, and a soft pillow to hide my face and cry. The pain that I felt from my throbbing, burning scalp felt like pins and needles in my head. It hurt too much to put a towel on it. It hurt to lie on my pillow.

"It hurts." I cried to my dear older brother as he did his best to comfort me. He tried to hug me, but it hurt me too much.

"It hurts so bad Jason!" I cried as my older brother gently patted my hand.

"Please let this end. Please make the hurt stop." I whispered to myself.

Living through that nightmare of almost drowning in the kitchen sink lasted for three nights.

-CHAPTER ELEVEN-

My First Swim Lesson

A few short months later, towards the end of spring, mother took us to the public swimming pool. Mother thought it would be good for me to learn how to swim before we went on our trip to father's house. Jason and I were going to visit our dad in Washington during summer vacation and throughout the next school year. Dad had just put in a pool that year so we could swim when the weather was warm. I was eight years old but I hadn't learned to swim yet and was completely content holding on to the side of the pool or just staying at the shallow end.

So I'm in the pool with mother, she wades out into the water and she takes a hold of me and before I know it, I'm on her hip and we're heading out to deeper waters. All the while, I'm pleading with her.

"No mommy. No, I don't want to learn. I'm not ready yet. Please! No!" She tells me to 'shush' and to trust her. There were plenty of other families there too. Mother held me out at arm's length and tried to teach me how to float. She attempted to get me to lay flat on top of the water all the while I clung to her arm for dear life.

"Just relax." She told me with this forced smile on her face. By then I was making a scene, begging her to stop and let me out of the water.

My only thoughts were of her trying to drown me at home, and the countless nights when I shook with fear when she walked into the bathroom while I was bathing. My eye watched her every move, as she got something out of the medicine cabinet. I didn't realize I was holding my breath until she left. Then I would let it out and try to calm back down. I continued to still plead and fuss.

"Stop it now." She yelled, "Just relax and trust me. I won't let you drown!" Mother finally gave up on the idea of teaching me how to float so she turned me over and told me to kick with my feet and paddle my arms as she held me at arm's length again. I was gasping for air and gulping water. Nothing seemed to be working and I was going under fast. I was scared and tired. I remember seeing all the people around me. They seemed content in watching the fiasco. "Oh, look that mother is teaching her little boy how to swim." Seemed to be their thoughts by the looks on their faces. Finally, I screamed,

"Help me, help me, please somebody help me. She's going to drown me!" 'Smack, Smack!' Mother hit my butt, removing the hand supporting my body and down I went swallowing more pool water. She got me up on top of the water again. She put on this act of fun and games and everything's okay. Big smiles and laughing

"Honey," She says, "Sweetie, just relax. You're going to be fine. Just relax and trust your mother. I won't let you drown." "Oh man," My mind races, "I'm dead, nobody believes me! I'm going to drown with all of these people around me... Did she just call me sweetie? Oh, no, I am so dead!" It was at that point, that I just gave up, I finally relaxed, or maybe it was just out of sheer exhaustion.

So that's how I learned to swim. I learned to swim, by giving up my fight for survival.

To this day, I go swimming from time to time I can only stay a short time in any body of water before I have to head for dry land. I even freak a little when I get water in my face.

Shortly after my "swimming lesson," I started to have strange dreams at night. In my dream, there was a black woman, she was a nun, and she came to our house to pick up Jason and I. We went to fun places like the park or to a pond so we could feed the ducks. She loved us very, very much. I felt so safe in those dreams and totally at peace with her. I would dream of her often after that, I guess it was my little world to escape and recharge my spirit. I remember having those dreams from the second grade through the sixth grade.

It seems funny now because mother was not a religious woman, but she used to send us boys to Sunday school, I guess mainly to get us out of the house on Sunday mornings. I fondly remember Jason and I wore matching white shirts with clip-on black bow ties. Mother kept a huge jug of 'Dippity Doo' hair gel in the bathroom and on Sunday mornings, we used enough of that in our hair to keep it in place for the whole week! Then we caught a ride on the "Joy Bus" that took us to and from church.

-CHAPTER TWELVE-

"So that's the Difference."

*D*uring our childhood, Jason and I spent most every summer vacation with our father and the rest of the Petra family in Washington in a small town called Aberdeen. In 1973, it was the first time we had stayed during the winter and went to school. I was in the third grade.

We grew up watching 'The Brady Bunch', 'Gilligan's Island', 'The Flintstones', and 'Speed Racer'. Sometimes when the weather was nice, we played outside. Father lived on fifty acres and most of it was pasture for the cows and horses. We had about an acre of trees, mostly alder trees. My Father, stepbrother Jr. and I built a Fort in this huge old pine tree. Jr. was two years younger than I was. Through the years, we put so many nails into that poor tree, it's a wonder it did not die of metal poisoning.

The winters in Washington were mostly wet and cold, so we stayed indoors a lot. One day, Leslie, my father's wife, told us to give our eyes a rest from watching too much television. So off we went to play in my half-sisters room that day. Rachel was three years old. In all my eight years, I had never been around so many frilly and ruffled things before. I wasn't much into her dolly things, but I thought her room looked pretty. We decided to play 'house'. Jason left because he said that he was way too old to play like sissies. JR and I didn't give it much thought.

"Oh, well, his loss." We said, as we took turns playing daddy and baby. Rachel played the mommy or baby, too. Since she was the youngest, she was the baby first. So we were playing away and then it was time to change her pretend diapers. I looked down at her private area and then I looked at JR and asked,

"Where's her Tallywacker?" I honestly looked around on the floor to see if it had fallen off somewhere.

"Silly, she don't have one. That's why she's a girl." He said. I thought it was odd, but I accepted his answer.

I wanted to investigate some more, so every chance I got, I was playing 'house' with Rachel. We took turns being the baby, until one day Leslie came into Rachel's room and caught us. I was on her bed with my pants down and Leslie just about hit the roof. I was up and out of my sister's room in a flash, while Leslie went for the rubber hose. I headed for my bedroom where I was told to go. The weapon of choice in the Petra household was a 3-foot section of garden hose. As mad as she was at me I was sure I'd get the life beat out of me. So when Leslie started in, I braced for the worse. She only hit me about three times, maybe four, then she stopped. I didn't know what to think about that. She didn't even leave a welt. I thought she was going to come back and discipline me some more but she never did and that confused me very much.

Leslie was very shook up and more upset than we were. She told us *never to* play that way again. She also said that she did not want father to know what she caught us doing. I did not know why she wanted it to be kept a secret. The whole experience left me feeling confused and very, very ashamed of myself. This was the beginning of many Petra Family Secrets

-CHAPTER THIRTEEN-

A Little Runaway

*A*fter spending the third grade school year and most of the summer with my father and the Petra family, Jason and I were back in California living under mother's roof once again. I had a tough time adjusting back into *her* routine of life. So much time had passed by, I saw how another household was run, and I liked it better than mother's tight ship.

It was about this time in my life that I started making it a habit of running away from home. Mother regularly said to me, as I would leave to start my day.

"Just wait until you get home from school, young man, you are in so much trouble!" That's how every school day started. So on those days I got absolutely nothing out of class, because I was so stressed out about the impending doom. I got so tired of worrying about it; I thought, "If I'm going to get in trouble tonight, then I just won't go home." So I went for extremely long walks after school. Sometimes I didn't come home until after dark. I got to the point where I didn't care if I got in trouble for running away or for whatever else I'd done wrong that morning. It seemed like a hopeless situation anyway.

Oddly enough, I never got in trouble for running away. One time when I finally did make my way home, mother said that she was sooo worried about me and told me that she had called friends in the neighborhood to ask if they had seen me. She also had Rodger drive around looking for me. "Yeah, right, I thought sarcastically, what a stupid lie!" I said to myself, "You don't love me. I'm a S.O.B., and a little piece of crap!" Sometimes I got so angry with her that by the time I made it home, I felt completely drained I was often too tired and hungry to even care.

On one occasion, mother called the police. The officer arrived just before dark. My mother knew me well enough to know that I would show up soon after sunset. She had already filled him in about my little independent outings. When I showed up on our front porch, the police officer took me for a little ride. He sat me in the back seat of his patrol car. It felt like I was in a cage. We rode in silence for a long time. The sounds from the police radio filled the air. I was getting a little worried and scared. That was quite an ordeal for a nine year old.

Eventually he turned his radio down and began to lecture me about how worried I had made my parents and that I was selfish for running away, and if I did it again that, he'd come back and put me in juvenile hall for a while.

"Yes sir." I replied. I knew I couldn't say anything else. I knew he would believe mother over me, which made me very sad.

He finally took me back home, there she was, the caring, and doting mother. She met us at the door, bent down to my eye level, and said,

"Now sweetie, I've heated up some soup for you. It's on the stove. You must be starved. Go on in and eat, then get ready for bed."

"Yes ma'am." I said as I walked into the house. Mother stayed on the porch and talked with the officer for a little while. My skin was crawling after witnessing, the class act performance that she had just put on for the officer. That night I began to feel even more isolated from the world around me. It seemed that mother had all her bases covered and I was trapped. "Oh, man, she called me 'Sweetie' again!" Those words made me shiver.

Even though I was under her clutches again, that was not the last time I ran away.

-CHAPTER FOURTEEN-

"What's In a Name?"

In the Halculm household, I was referred to as 'Blockhead'. Rodger came up with that nickname one night as we watched 'Charlie Brown and the Great Pumpkin'. Jason had a nickname too. It was 'Blabbermouth', because he got into so many fights at school for running off at the mouth. Even some of our parent's friends called us 'Blabbermouth' and 'Blockhead,' too. Everybody thought it was so cute. I'd smile because the grownups were smiling. Smiles were nice; they meant all was well. Smiles meant I was safe because everyone was happy. I didn't like being called Blockhead. Then again, didn't every beloved child have a nickname? Even our little brother Jack was called 'Charlie Brown'. Our step-dad would call out in fun "Good grief Charlie Brown!" Jack would just laugh like crazy. He thought it was great. Jack should be so lucky to be called Charlie Brown, but then Jack was born mentally retarded, and what would people think if they heard a handicapped child being called a degrading nickname by his own parents anyway?

I do recall a few times when mother called me 'son' in an endearing way, and not in reference to a S.O.B. I was nine years old, when I developed epilepsy. I will never forget my first seizure; I was awake in bed when it happened. I shook and jerked so hard that my brothers woke up. They hollered for our parents to come quick. After the seizure passed, my mother held me and comforted me because I was so scared. As she cradled me, I thought, "Wow, mommy really, really loves me. See, she does care. Mommy really does love me. I will never doubt her love for me again."

"I love you mommy." I said to her.

"Shhh... I love you too, son." She replied.

That night, I got to ride in an ambulance and mother was my hero.

I continued to have night seizures several times a year. I hated going to bed I always wondered when the next episode would hit me. I endured the seizures for eight years. The last one occurred when I was sixteen. Thank goodness, I grew out of them. The seizures seemed to stop as suddenly as they began. To my knowledge, nobody knows why they happen or who's going to have an attack.

After that first seizure mother kept a clothespin by my bed, just in case I started to swallow my tongue during one of my seizures. I knew she loved me so... as time went by I used to hold that wooden clothespin gently in my hands and recall the night my mother was somebody else. Someone who loved her son. Unfortunately, my illusions of having a loving, nurturing mother were short lived and sadly, the beatings continued.

~

There is a sad experience in the book, 'Necessary Losses' that made me think of my own feelings toward my mother, quote;

"A young boy lies in a hospital bed. He is frightened and in pain. Burns cover 40% of his small body. Someone has dowsed him with alcohol and then, unimaginably, has set him on fire.

He cries for his mother.

His mother has set him on fire.

It doesn't matter whether she hurts or hugs. Separation from mother is worse than being in her arms when the bombs are exploding. Separation from mother is sometimes worse than being with her when she is the bomb."

The story saddened me deeply and yet it helped me to make sense of my own feelings. It helped me to see that I was normal to still love my mother and so desperately want her to love me and to be close to her even though she was the bomb.

-CHAPTER FIFTEEN-

Mother Has Me in Stitches

Mother was a perfectionist. Her home was always very clean and orderly. Every closet and shelf was kept organized to her specifications.

One day, when I was nine, mother asked me to get a lid to fit on a container of food she had made and put in the refrigerator earlier that day. Mother was not one to give easy assignments or directions. She made everything so complicated. It was as if she wanted us to fail, to give her a reason to get mad.

I couldn't remember all the steps to follow in order to find that proper lid without messing up her cupboards. I was not allowed to open up the fridge and just look at the bowl that needed the lid. So there I was standing there lost. Mother had already repeated herself twice, and had me repeat her directions exactly as she said them. They were so long and confusing. I said the words, but that's all I could do. By the time I reached the kitchen I was so anxious and scared of displeasing her, my little rattled brain went blank.

Time was running out and I knew she was about to reach her boiling point. Slowly, I went back into the living room where mother was busy ironing and watching her soaps on television.

"Mom, I can't find it." I said, defeated.

Mother grabbed me by my ear and hurried me back into the dining room. She had run out of patience and evidently, I had pushed her too far.

"Get your ass back in there and get that damn lid now!" She told me sternly. Then she threw me into the kitchen.

I literally flew through the air; and, as I came crashing down; my left temple connected with the corner of the open cabinet door. As I scurried to my feet and tried to look for the lid, my vision became blurry and my head started hurting. I collapsed to my knees. Blood started to trickle down my cheek and onto my shirt. I start to breathe heavy and the tears started to mix with the blood running down my face.

Mother must have seen the blood, because she came into the kitchen. I heard her approaching but couldn't see her. "Oh no, she's getting closer. No, no, no." I thought to myself! As I flinched, I said to her,

"Oh, please mommy, no more, no more please. I'll find the right lid. I'll be good!"

"Hold still." Mother said as she inspected the cut. Then she hurried to get a washcloth and a small towel with ice.

"Here, let me clean it up." She said while she gently pressed the washcloth it to my temple. Then she said, "Okay, I'll get the car keys. Let's go. We have to have a doctor look at you. Here, hold this." She handed me the towel with ice. My head was still spinning and throbbing and yet I thought, "Who was this woman. She is a saint! My mother does love me. I hurt myself and now she has come to my side. She's taking care of me."

On the way to the emergency room, mother told me,

"Okay, now, I want you to tell the doctor that you and Jason were rough housing around in the kitchen, and that you got hurt on an open cabinet door. Okay, do you understand; you and your brother was horse playing. Alright?" She asked again.

"Okay mommy." I said, while truly not understanding anything that was going on. My thoughts were racing, "Why does mommy want me to say that? I was bad and did not do as I was told. Landing the way I did was an accident. I should have closed the door. I shouldn't get mother upset like I always do."

We finally got to the hospital and mother parked the car. Once again, we reviewed my explanation to the doctor. I repeated what she told me, and then she said,

"That's right, and after we are done seeing the doctor, how about us stopping on the way home and get us an ice cream cone. Wouldn't you like that?" I nodded yes.

Sure enough, after getting eight stitches put in less than a half inch away from my eye; and, a stern talking to from the doctor about the dangers of horse playing in the house, we were off to get some ice cream and back home just before my step-dad got home. Mother quickly put dinner together and since the story worked so well at the hospital, she decided to carry it through that evening by telling step-dad the same thing. Rodger wasn't always aware of what mother was doing to us boys. He was a little upset with Jason and me for costing him another hospital bill. Mother tried to smooth things over.

"But, boys will be boys." She told him with a smile as she put another helping of his favorite dinner on his plate.

Lend Me Your Ear

Mother's house was so organized that she even rotated the linens, so that they would all be equally used and wear evenly. One laundry day, she was in a particularly foul mood. There were four stacks of linens on the sofa ready to be put away. She gave me explicit directions; she told me that half of one stack was to go under a couple of towels that were already on the shelf in the bathroom above the toilet. Some washcloths had to go on a certain side behind one of two stacks of something else, and the rest of the linens went in the utility closet.

Her directions kept getting longer and longer and I was starting to get overwhelmed. But I never dared tell her that I didn't understand her instructions because I was scared to death she'd get mad at me. So I tried my best, which was never good enough.

As I stepped onto the toilet seat, I managed to remember where the first set of towels went. But halfway through with the second stack, my brain went blank and I stood there wishing something would come back to my memory. For quite some time I was there just stressing, because I knew that mother's patience was wearing thin.

Moments later, all hell broke loose. Mother came charging into the bathroom and we stood face to face. She proceeded to scream the directions at me slowly and methodically. By now, I was visibly shaking and trying my best to balance everything in my hands and keep from falling off the toilet seat.

"Why... in... the... name... of... God... can't... you... listen... to... what... I... tell... you?" Mother yelled. Then she took her left hand and placed it firmly on the side of my blubbering face. Then with all of her might, she slapped me with her right hand. She hit me so hard that I heard nothing but a loud deafening ringing in my left ear. After that, she grabbed me by the hair and threw me to the ground, while the laundry flew everywhere.

"Pick it up you deaf Son of a Bitch!" She spat, as she took me by the ear, and led me around to every piece of linen I had dropped.

"Now, pick up this one and this one over here. Now, let's go down the hallway to the utility closet. Come on, hurry up!" She furiously said as she walked at a fast pace.

My ears were still ringing, and my equilibrium was off balance, so I kept losing my footing. Mother still had a death grip on my ear as she dragged me down the hall, slamming me against the walls on the way. Then she pitched me into the utility closet door. After I finally put the rest of the laundry away, she dragged me back down the hall and into the living room. Then she grabbed a fist full of my hair in one hand and my ear in the other while she literally spun me around in a circle through the air.

Each time she lost her grip, I went tumbling. Then she grabbed another handful of hair and it started again. As I crashed down, she came over and started yanking at my ears and shaking me like a pit bull would do with a rag doll.

"Since your ears don't seem to be working, I'll just pull the sons of bitches off!" Mother ranted on. I was crying and terrified. She continued to spin me around the living room again; but this time she held on to both ears, I was flying about a foot off the ground and completely at her mercy. Mother kept losing her grip so I continued to crash into the walls and furniture. The blood from my torn ears flew everywhere. Eventually Mother got tired of losing her grip, so she got two washcloths and proceeded to successfully pick me up by my ears again and spin me around several more times until the blood-soaked washcloths finally slipped off; and, for the last time I crashed down at the side of the sofa. I cowered as she came toward me. I felt trapped; there was nowhere to hide. She bent down, took my head with both of her hands, then with all her strength, she slapped both of my ears at the same time. She continued to do that again and again and again and again.

I knew she was still screaming at me because I could see her lips moving, but all that I could hear was the ringing in my ears. I was in so much pain that I couldn't feel the hurt she was inflicting on me anymore. I just went numb. The next thing I remembered was being picked up and thrown down the hall. She told me to clean myself up!

As I stood at the bathroom sink, exhausted, I attempted to comb my hair that was matted with blood from my bleeding scalp and ears. It was extremely painful. I had to brace myself on the sink to keep from falling. Still crying and trembling as I took a cool, wet cloth and dabbed my ears. It took forever for the bleeding to slow down and finally stop.

I faintly heard mother in the other room yelling at me to hurry up and finish my chores. The trash needed to be taken out. Then she told me to go to my room and stay there until dinner. I could sense that she was ticked off at me for messing up the house. There was blood and hair everywhere, the walls, carpet, and furniture. There was even blood spattered on the cat, because he was caught in the crossfire before he could scurry out of harm's way.

By the time I made it to bed, I was totally drained emotionally and hurting beyond belief. Somehow, I was able to fall asleep for a while. Just before dinner, I woke up with bloodstains on my pillow. Mother summoned me to the bathroom. She had calmed down enough to clean my ears, put gauze and tape on them. Then she cleaned off the areas on my head where she had pulled so much hair out in sections. It felt like someone had tried to scalp me. I could tell Mother was still angry, because she wasn't very gentle in combing out the dried blood. My ears continued to ring for five or six days. The skin on my ears had split from the top front of the ear, all the way down the back and around my ear lobe. My wounds eventually scabbed over. My ears were scabbed on the inside too, where mother had gripped them so hard that she had pierced through them with her fingernails.

It seemed like just as I'd start to heal up, mother would go into a violent rage again, grab me by the ears and hair, and take me for another excruciating spin around the living room. This routine went on for about two or three more weeks. She finally stopped, because I was missing too many days of school.

When I was finally able to go to school, I had to keep my stocking cap on to hide my ears and bald patches. With the shape I was in, I was so thankful it was wintertime; I would have been so embarrassed and ashamed of myself for being such a bad boy. I thought, "If only I had behaved better or if only I had listened better. Then mother would be happy. Then she'd love me."

"Oh Look, I'm not alone!"

Sometime after my ears healed, mother had me stay up past my bedtime, to watch one of those shows like '20/20' or '60 Minutes'. They were doing a story on a family like ours. The family allowed them to put hidden cameras throughout their house.

After a time, the parents were shown screaming and beating their kids. I don't remember what the news reporter had to say. I only recall watching the television and wondering, "Why on earth did mother single me out to watch this show?" I was confused. She turned it off towards the end and said,

"See there, you think you're so abused? How would you like to live in *that* household?" I was dumbfounded by her question. I'm sure now that she turned the TV off just before the part where they took their children away. I wonder if they had a Department of Family Protective Services back in 1975?

As I made my way to bed that night I thought, "Hey, I really am not alone. I'm not the only one that has it so rough at home. There are other bad little boys and girls out there getting disciplined just like me."

-CHAPTER SIXTEEN-

"A Ten Year Old Homosexual?"

*T*he Halculm family had a new addition. My baby brother, Jerry, was born. We also moved to a bigger house to accommodate our growth. So there we were, with a new home, new neighbors, new schools and new friends.

Halloween had come and gone. I had done something wrong yet again and was grounded from 'Trick-or-Treating.' At least I was spared the humiliation of having to pass out candy again. Mother probably didn't want to give a bad impression to our new neighbors, and for that, I was grateful.

Thanksgiving came and went without a hitch however, Christmas time was a different story. I found myself in trouble for something I did or didn't do, and my parents played it up all the way, saying, "Bad little boys get nothing from Santa." Then Rodger put a lump of coal in my stocking and they made me watch as the rest of the family opened their presents from "Saint Nick." Even though I was old enough to know there was no Santa Claus, I was still made to feel worthless.

Christmas vacation was finally over and school resumed. I always looked forward to going back to school because it was a safe haven for me away from the storm. I was in the fifth grade and an average student, never in much trouble. I was not into sports or running with the popular crowd. I had a few friends, mostly girls. They're not so rough when they play and a lot more mellow to be around.

During one recess, a group of boys were bullying me. They were teasing me because I would never play football with the guys.

"Four square is a girl's game. Only boys who are wusses play with girls." They jeered as they shoved me and hit me in the back then in the stomach. The bullies were mainly sixth graders and some fifth grade students who were cool enough to hang out with the older ones.

Finally, one kid came forward from the back of the crowd. He was a sixth grader and his name was Gamin. He stood taller than most of all the other kids. Probably because he was thirteen, Gamin was supposed to be in Junior High, but he got held back.

"All right, knock it off!" Gamin said as he came up to me and helped me up from the ground. I was grateful but a bit embarrassed. I was banged up pretty bad, but mostly humiliated.

"Thanks." I said as the crowd broke up and returned to playing.

"Do you want to walk over to the water fountain and get a drink?" Gamin asked.

"Sure." I replied. By the time I took a drink and tucked in the back of my shirt, I was beginning to calm down; I wiped a silent tear from my eye.

Then Gamin and I sat down against a wall and started talking. That was the first of many recesses we spent together. Sometimes we were with the other children, but mainly by ourselves. I liked the fact that he was a sixth grader, not only to look out for me, but I felt he was a true buddy.

One day when we met at recess, Gamin said,

"Hey, I got to take a piss."

"Yeah, me too." I said, and off to the boy's restroom we ran. We were the only ones there.

I was just finishing when Gamin, from the next stall over, yelled over to me.

"Hey, come here!" I looked in on him as he was still standing and facing the toilet.

"What?" I asked.

"Come here and look." Gamin said as he moved over so I could see. His penis was erect and he was playing with himself.

"Can you do this?" Gamin asked.

"Do what?" I replied. I was struck with wonder at what Gamin was doing, and why he wanted me to watch. I immediately felt uncomfortable.

"Pull yours out, Jim."

"Okay." I said sheepishly. I stuck mine out and then Gamin fondled me.

"Here, touch mine." He said. I was fidgeting and I reluctantly touched his. Then all of the sudden we heard kids running to get a drink and to use the restrooms. Gamin told me,

"Don't tell anyone what we were doing. It'll be our little secret."

"Okay." I said. "I won't tell." I didn't know what we were doing anyway, but I knew it was a secret. Moreover, if I was good at *anything*, I was certainly good at keeping secrets.

When we met the next day Gamin said,

"Come on, I'll show you a secret hideout."

"Great." I said. We ran out behind the cafeteria and behind some bushes that grew big and thick alongside the school building that ran by the road. This area was definitely out of bounds for children. We stopped once we got to a little opening where we could squeeze into, all the while we were huffing and puffing and out of breath. It was definitely an adrenalin rush from being somewhere, we knew was off limits.

Gamin talked me into pulling down my pants and when I did, he bent down and started sucking my penis. I was definitely uncomfortable about what was going on at first. Those new feelings I felt were odd to me, but definitely pleasing.

After a minute, Gamin stood up then pulled out his own penis.

"Okay, now you suck on my dick." He said to me. I felt obligated to comply because he had just sucked on mine, and I did not want to lose his friendship, and he saved me from the bullies. Besides, hanging out with him was cool because he was two years older than I was. So from that day this became a daily ritual for Gamin and I during our noon recess.

During this same period, mother began to notice I was spending a lot of time touching and fondling myself. I did it subconsciously. It seemed to comfort me. Sometimes when mother tucked us in at bedtime, she caught me playing with myself. She pulled down my blankets and my pajamas, and then she yelled,

"Quit touching your Tallywacker or I'll get a butcher knife and cut it off." While yelling, she flicked my little erection with her fingers several times. That really hurt it was extremely embarrassing. She did the same to Jason. I could only imagine the humiliation he felt, just turning thirteen.

However, one day when Gamin and I were together, I guess he thought it would be cool to show his friends what he got a fifth grader to do for him. So as usual, we met at our usual hideout and I started to undo my pants when Gamin interrupted me,

"No, don't do that yet. Here, I want you to suck on my dick for a while."

"Okay." I replied. So I got down on my knees, started to do it, when all of a sudden, I heard a rush of kids come yelling, and laughing. I got up fast and ran out from behind the bushes and ran as fast as I could to the boy's restroom.

Well, in no time at all the word was out to the rest of the children at recess that Gamin got me to suck his penis. All the kids were whispering, giggling, and jeering at me. The news finally got around to my teacher and she personally took me to the principal's office. 'Arlington Heights Elementary School, Mr. Kane, Principal', was written on his door. He was a very large fat man with a flat top haircut. He had a thunderous voice, which demanded attention when he spoke. I entered his office as my teacher left to go back to class. Then Mr. Kane's secretary called Gamin in.

Mr. Kane calmly asked Gamin and I what was going on. We sat there, fidgeting and mumbling something. Then, Mr. Kane started speaking. As he spoke, he continued to get louder and louder saying something about us being homosexuals, and how we carried on was a disgrace. He said he was going to have our parents come down and what an embarrassment we were to the school and to our parents. Mr. Kane must have said the word 'homosexual' about seven or eight times at least. I didn't have a clue what he was talking about; it must've had something to do with what Gamin and I were doing together, and it was something very, very, very bad.

My mother finally showed up, and Mr. Kane stepped out to talk with her. As he did, Gamin apologized for what he'd done to me then said,

"Now, when Mr. Kane comes back in, we just tell him we only got together just three or four times and that's it."

"Okay." I whispered, not looking up.

I was thinking of how upset Mr. Kane was and that surely it

would mean death for me when I got home. However, oddly enough, when we finally left his office, Mother and I drove home in silence. When we got home, I was just grounded to my room for the two weeks I was expelled from school. After that day, mother never mentioned anything about the incident. I went back to school and finished the fifth grade with very little problems. There was a memo passed through the faculty about what had happened. Before I was allowed back into class, my teacher gave a stern warning about not teasing me and for everyone to drop the whole ordeal and carry on as normal. Gamin never did return. He was having trouble with school even before all this took place. So Gamin's father decided to try home schooling.

Mr. Kane told my mother that he thought it would be best if I could change school systems and start new somewhere in order to put the whole situation behind me. So when summer came, Jason and I made our yearly trip up to Washington but at the end of summer, Jason left and I stayed. When I went to school, I was glad to see that the same friends I had back when I was in the third grade were still around. Some of us even had the same sixth grade teacher.

Jason didn't fare as well. He returned to school where he wasn't just a new rookie ninth grader, but the mean kids would tease and call him. 'The brother of a dick sucker.'

From then on there was an ever-present wedge between Jason and I. Jason was never able to live my reputation down. Despite all of the effort he put into doing his best at sports and trying to make a name for himself. I can't help but wonder if this experience contributed to Jason's drug abuse and dropping out of high school his junior year. I blame myself for this. Regrettably, we were never as close as we were while growing up. Sadly, it was never the same.

-CHAPTER SEVENTEEN-

Birth of the Mask

Grandpa and Grandma Petra's holiday traditions were like most families.

And like other families with spouses and parents of their own, the holiday meals and festivities were split between one in-law's home and the others. I guess that's why there is so much traveling and traffic during those times of the year.

For my family, it meant having to drive to Grandma and Grandpa Petra's house, who lived about two hundred miles from the rest of their family. They had a house with a hundred acres near the Pacific Coast. Grandpa worked on the docks as a longshoreman out of Port Angeles. Before and after work he would tend to his cattle. There was always something to do on the farm, whether it was feeding cattle, chasing cows back into their proper fields or mending fences. He always tried to find time to squeeze in a little fishing or crabbing down at the Bay. Grandma usually accompanied him to the Bay on most of his trips, but as time went on, their outings together, became fewer and Grandpa went by himself more and more.

Grandma Petra's health went downhill, or so it seemed. She went to the doctors and they ran various tests. Even the specialists were clueless as to what was wrong with her. They gave her several different prescriptions. Some worked well, while others did not. Grandpa did his very best to take care of Grandma. But like most caregivers, it was discouraging for him. He continued to work to provide for his wife and Everett, their youngest child, who was about four years older than I was.

After a few years into her illness, Grandpa Petra eventually noticed a pattern. She was sick for weeks at a time. But whenever a special event came up, she was ready to party. It was as if she wore a mask. She enjoyed her family get-togethers very much, and hosted most of them herself. Knowing she was not in good health, her children were always willing to pitch in and help.

"No, no, I can get it!" Grandma insisted, while laughing and carrying on in good spirits. The energy level to maintain such a facade always came with a price. Grandpa knew all too well, that all of the festivities would set her back for at least two weeks after everyone was gone and life went back to normal. Whether Grandma was truly physically sick, or was it just emotional, I don't know. Maybe she was unhappy with Grandpa Petra and just didn't want to do the things he wanted to do. Maybe she was suffering from depression. All I know for sure is that the vein of pride runs deep within the Petra family and that, to me Grandma was the first generation in my family to wear the 'Happy Mask' and the 'Everything is Just Fine Mask'.

Unfortunately, these Masks were handed down to the next generation. The "Masks" gave birth to other "Masks" for the sole purpose of covering dysfunctional relationships, family secrets, toxic shame, guilt, and regrets, along with other embarrassing scars. By the time those dreadful fake Masks were handed down to me, they were well worn and extremely comfortable. The Masks had such a natural feel to them; we did not even realize we were wearing them. Our true feelings, individuality, personal opinions, and values were hidden behind them.

'Bradshaw on the Family' says, *"Denying our emotions are a way that causes us to lose control over them. Once repressed and denied you no longer have your emotions, they have you."*

The burdens of the Masks were very heavy. Pride was the secret adhesive, that pride kept the Masks together, strong, ever present and in place.

Learning a God Condemning Practice

It wasn't long after completing the fifth grade, and moving from my mother's in California, that my father and Leslie got custody of me through the court system, so they wouldn't have to pay child support for me.

I started the sixth grade and before long, Thanksgiving was upon us and we were on our way to stay the four-day weekend with the Petra's. Sometime during the long car ride, we kids got that lecture, number one hundred and fifty-seven, the one about being on our very best behavior or you'll be in sooo much trouble when we got back home.'

My dad had a little brother named Everett. He was four years older than I was. My stepbrother JR, age ten, and I, liked to sleep in our sleeping bags in Uncle Everett's bedroom. We loved looking through his large collection of comic books. On night, after reading through a few comics, and after he made sure his bedroom door was closed secure, Uncle Everett talked JR and I into joining him in his bed to look at a special magazine. I was on one side and JR on the other. Then Everett whispered,

"Okay, Shhh....keep it down so I can hear if someone's coming." He adjusted the covers around us, and then pulled out a high glossy picture magazine that he had stashed under his pillow. JR and I had never seen a magazine like that one. It had pictures of women wearing very little, or no clothes at all. Their bodies looked all oily and they had tons of make-up on.

"Pretty great, don't you think?" Everett whispered. JR agreed, saying,

"Yeah, NEAT!" As he grabbed the magazine from Everett.

While we took turns looking at that odd picture book, Everett pulled out his penis and started playing with himself; the pictures excited Everett, but I only felt bewildered. That was the first time I had seen a naked woman. Before that, I had never given it much thought. It didn't do much for me... not as it did for Uncle Everett. After he cleaned himself off, he asked us if we had ever masturbated. We said we hadn't, so he showed us how. As he fondled us, I thought, "Here I go again." It had only been a year since my experience with Gamin in the schoolyard. I didn't mind though, because I thought, "This is different. Uncle Everett loves me. We're family, and he wouldn't hurt me. I like the attention and I feel loved." These were some of the many thoughts, which were swimming around in my head.

Little did I know then these events would lead to a life-long battle with masturbation.

So Uncle Everett introduced JR and I to a couple of demoralizing habits. The degradation of women; objectively viewing them through pornography and the god-condemning practice of masturbation. Uncle Everett was not the first to abuse me sexually however his timing was impeccable. My sexual development was just awakening. Unfortunately, I continued to fuel these desires through masturbation.

We did not have access, nor did we even consider bringing pornography into my father's house. So I sought out the next best thing available to feed my fantasies. We always had the latest 'Wish Books', catalogs of major department stores at home. Those three-inch thick glossy books were the closest JR and I were going to get to seeing women in underclothes or swimming apparel to satisfy our sexual fantasies, of course 'National Geographic' came in handy too.

Leslie found the catalogs in JR's room on many occasions, stashed under his bed.

"I was looking at the toys and school clothes." He proclaimed. However, JR sought them out for the same reason I did throughout our teenage years.

One time, I must not have paid much attention while I was attending to my private business; apparently, Leslie caught me in the act. She didn't confront me personally. I could only imagine the chain of events that followed.

~ No doubt, she must have been shocked and revolted by what she saw. She probably stewed over it and prayed for a healthy day or two wondering what on earth she was going to do about her discovery. She probably thought, "Certainly this child of my husband's is a hopeless case, and this situation goes way beyond my job as his step-mother. Oh, but I better make sure that behavior doesn't rub off on JR"~

Soon after that, JR got me alone in the living room and declared,

"I don't know when you did it, but mom came into my room last night and she was very upset. She was crying and she asked me if I knew how to masturbate and if I had learned it from you. Of course, I said "no." Then she told me that she knew you masturbated, and she hoped that I would never even start such a god condemning practice. I told her I wasn't aware of you doing that and then said I would never do it because that would be gross. Then she hugged me and left, still sobbing on the way out of my room. Jimmy, you had better be more careful. You'll end up getting into really hot water if you don't watch it."

Since JR was very sneaky, my step-mother never doubted him. She put on the 'Blind Mask'.

-CHAPTER EIGHTEEN-

Puppy Love

I fell in love with my first girlfriend when I was in the sixth grade. Cassy and I were in the same class. She was taller than I was, and she had jet-black hair that flowed past her waist. She was so beautiful and I had a crush on her like you wouldn't believe. I just knew she was the girl that I was going to marry. Interestingly enough, Leslie was tall and had long straight jet-black hair too. I think one reason I was proud that Cassy was my girlfriend was so my father would see that he and I liked the same kind of girls…always looking for approval.

My father and Leslie approved of Cassy. I was even allowed to take her roller-skating with us on Sunday night as a family. They thought it was cute. I was mortified that my parents would do something to embarrass me in front of Cassy. I was so extremely nervous that I must have sweated ten gallons from my hands alone.

Later Leslie discouraged any kind of opposite sex relationships from developing. Even years later, when Rachel was almost seventeen years old, my dad went behind Leslies back to help his daughter date the boy which she later married at age eighteen.

Cassy and I were an item all through the sixth grade and on into the seventh. Then something changed. She was no longer happy just holding hands and walking her to classes. She wanted to move our relationship up to the next level. She wanted me to start kissing her. "No way!" I said to myself. I was in a spot! My step-mother had taught us that kissing leads to petting, necking, and then uncontrolled sexual desires meant only for married people. Having sex and getting a girl pregnant was definitely a carnal sin. Even *thinking* of such a thing was a sin. So there I was,

"No way, I can't kiss you!" I told Cassy, "I'd be in so much trouble with my parents if they were to find out!" Well, she was just too sophisticated for me after that. She broke up with me and I was crushed.

For the next few years, I liked other girls at school, but I was too afraid and ashamed to start anything serious with them.

-CHAPTER NINETEEN-

Sex Education (Part One)

Our family never talked about sex. In fact, if any television program showed anything more than a quick kiss, Leslie changed the channel. Sex outside of marriage was considered dirty and sinful. Even immoral thoughts were condemnable.

Therefore, it took me quite by surprise when my Father brought the subject up one cold winter day. JR, who had just turned twelve, and I was thirteen, were out chopping wood with Father. We were cutting and stacking away, when out of the blue Father asked us,

"Hey guys. When you take a bath or shower, do you wash your balls?" I was floored. I thought, "Where did that come from? Are we in trouble? Do we stink? Why is he asking us this? Did step-mom tell him something?" JR and I both paused for a long time.

"When you boys take a shower, do you guys wash your balls?" Father repeated himself.

"Well… yes dad." We both said, utterly embarrassed.

"How do you do that?" He asked, "You got a zipper on your bag to take them out? Ha, Ha, Ha…" He thought it was the funniest joke ever. We laughed too, not because the joke was funny, but because JR and I were relieved, we weren't in trouble. So that was it. That was the extent of our sex education from our father.

Sex Education (Part Two)

One day at school, during the seventh grade, I was looking at an eighth grader's health book. There were these drawings close-up pictures of a woman giving birth. I stared at the picture for a long time, but couldn't figure out what part of the woman's body it was. Finally, I sheepishly asked the eighth grader some questions. I didn't even know him very well but I was so grateful he took me serious and quietly explained it all to me. Up until that time, I always thought that babies were cut out of the mother's stomach, because my own mother had a scar where she said Jack and Jerry came from.

"So that's where babies come from?" I whispered as the class bell rang. He told me everything. Even the bleeding thing when girls get old enough. They grow hair down there, have a cycle, and get pregnant if they kiss a person too long. That was it. We said our goodbyes and I had all this newfound knowledge to think about and absorb.

-CHAPTER TWENTY-

A 360-Degree Cycle – From Victim to Victimizer

When we had family gatherings at Uncle Dan Petra's house, all of us kid's played games in the basement of their home. Uncle Everett, although he was sixteen, played along with us.

Uncle Everett always wanted us, his nieces and nephews, to play 'house' or 'doctor.' These games always led to touching each other in our privates. Uncle Everett, JR, and I would take turns playing the male roles. Rachel, who was seven, Jessica, six years old and her little sister Erica who was five, played the female roles. In time, I was catching on to Uncle Everett's tactics; and, when we left to go to our various homes after such visits, eventually I talked Rachel into playing "house" by ourselves. We would head out to the tree fort and this was our house. Our playing house too always led to sexual touching that our uncle taught us. During these times I thought, "Sex is wrong, but I'm only fondling her. I like playing 'house' with my sister. This is okay because I'm showing Rachel that I love her. She likes what we're doing. I'm not hurting her. I like the attention, I feel loved. We're family. She does not have hair down there so that means she is too young to get pregnant. I'm not having sex with her anyways; we're only touching each other." Playing house with Rachel made me feel warm, happy, and somehow secure. Rachel and I continued to play house for six months until, unbeknown to us; Leslie followed us out to the tree one day and caught us, literally, with our pants down. We were spanked and lectured then spanked again by father when he got home, and I was grounded to my room.

Normally when we'd get in trouble and grounded in the Petra House, it would be for a maximum of a two-week stretch. About two and a half weeks of being confined to my room, I asked father if I could get off being grounded. I thought that maybe he had forgotten about me. He looked at me puzzled and realized that I really didn't understand the severity of my actions. He didn't try to explain it to me any better, he just said,

"No, you're still grounded. You need to think about what you did for a little longer." I was grounded for a little over six weeks. During this period, I finally realized that what I had done was *really* bad. I wasn't about to do that again if it meant being grounded to my room forever.

Rachel and I were never left alone again. That's how it stayed as long as I lived under my father's roof. I felt bad about being condemned and never trusted ever again. However, as time passed by, it just came to be a way of life. Looking back now, I realize that sadly, I continued to find ways to victimize my half-sister as well as her girlfriends. I'd watch them from my bedroom window as they played in our pool. I thought, "Wow this is wonderful! What a sneak I am." As I observed them through the crack in the curtain, I masturbated in the darkness of my room. I convinced myself that what I was doing was okay because nobody knew about it and that I wasn't hurting anyone. Now I reflect back and I realize just how really sick and twisted my thinking and actions were. Rachel was no dummy, there were times when she would glance up at my window and see the curtain move then tell her friends that she didn't want to swim anymore, and they'd go off to play somewhere else away from my watchful eyes. I cannot even imagine the hell she went through having to live in the same house with a perverted Peeping Tom for a brother and making her skin crawl just being in the same room with me.

What a very sad way to have to grow up and live under those conditions. Prisoner in your own home. Having to pull the shades down continually, for fear of someone might be outside lurking in the shadows, praying for a glance at you. Sadly, regrettably, that someone was me. Regrettably, I also victimized my stepbrother. One evening, JR and I were playing in his room. I was feeling brotherly and close to him. I was also feeling sexually stimulated, as I was twenty-five hours a day anyway. As we were hanging out and being boys, I thought, "You know, I sure am glad JR and I have been getting along lately. He's really great when he ain't telling on me. I want to show him something I bet Uncle Everett hadn't taught him. I want to show JR that I really care about him and that I love him." I thought about what Gamin taught me in the bushes behind the cafeteria.

"Come on, I know you'll like it, you'll see." I told him so he reluctantly let me put his penis in my mouth for a couple of seconds.

"No, no more. This is freaking me out." He declared.

"Okay, okay! I'm sorry; okay just don't tell on me, alright?" I said. I was hoping if he liked it, then he wouldn't tell on me. But, it didn't work out that way. I thought, "Oh no! Okay, time to make sure I stay on his good side for a while or I'll be in trouble again!" I was worried and filled with anxiety for days after that. "Stupid hormones, stupid Tallywacker, stupid blockhead…" I said, condemning myself.

-CHAPTER TWENTY ONE-

"I Can Rationalize My Way To Doing Just About Anything!"

*S*ome months had passed since Rachel and I was caught playing house. My hormones, however, were still raging out of control. Masturbation became my favorite pastime.

One day JR and I were on our way out to the tree fort and he stopped to visit our pet cow, named Bluca. She always greeted us because she knew we probably had some grain for her. As we were petting her, JR told me he wanted to show me something.

"Look at this." He said as he lifted up her tail.

"Yeah, so what?" I said. Then he explained that if I got a five-gallon bucket I could stand on it and be able to stick my penis in her. He told me it was better than masturbating. I thought, "Man that is so gross!" However, as time went by, the more I thought about it, the more I began to reason. "Hey, why not. I'm tired of rubbing myself raw, and there's no way I can get her pregnant. I wouldn't be hurting anybody, and if JR's doing it I guess I can try it once." I was very horny and curious. Regrettably, I did it a few times and every time after wards, I was thoroughly grossed-out and disgusted with myself.

Then, one day for some unknown reason, JR decided to tell father what I was doing with our cow. Even though I had seen him do it too, I never told on JR

Years earlier Jason and I agreed we would never tattle on each other because we were punished enough as it was. Why add to it. So I carried that thinking through my teen years. Nobody would've believed me anyways, it was always one-sided storytelling at our house. Whatever JR or Rachel said became the gospel truth. Father had decided not to tell Leslie about Bluca and me. I guess he figured she barely made it through the ordeal with Rachel and me. So yet, another secret was added to the Petra foundation.

My father grounded me for a couple of weeks. My gross actions were kept private. I was so grateful because I was humiliated enough as it was. I felt so ashamed of myself, like I was scum of the earth. As I look back now I can see the self-disgust and inner pain just piling up within me. I definitely needed professional help but my parents were too proud to consider the possibility of seeking professional help for me, even if they had the money to waste on me.

~

I realize that this story was probably much more information than anyone would want to know, but I'm reminded again of the affirmation, "You are only as sick as your secrets." For too many years, my secrets had done nothing but keep me stuck in my toxic shame and loathsome self-disgust. By telling my stories, as utterly humiliating as this one, they stop having a hold on me and I can finally move forward. In trauma healing, I have learned that the more you share, the more others will share with you.

Therefore, I used to be filled with self-loathing and it kept me isolated, yet I have experienced a couple of things on my journey towards inner healing,

1) I have found others who used to view themselves in a self-destructive way and if they can gain self-worth, respect, and dignity, so can I.

2) You might be surprised to hear the person next to you has done something in their past that was equal to, if not a little bit more bizarre, then what you have.

By freeing each other of those ever present destructive Masks we all seem to have which keep us stuck behind our secrets and in our sickness.

Therefore, I encourage anyone who is serious about trauma healing to find someone safe to share your secrets with, doing so it will help us all to succeed in stopping the cycle of abuse.

"Shame dissipates the moment you realize you're not alone."

Rage Passed On To the Next Generation

I was still thirteen when this next incident took place. Leslie tried to reason with me using the scriptures whenever I'd get in trouble. To me, all I saw was her Bible as an extension of her arm, followed by a lot of weeping and nagging. Back then, I just knew that lecture number twenty-seven through two thousand and four was tailor made for me. I thought, "I have more rules to follow than those Israelites of old. Did Moses whine as much as mom?"

One day we were arguing about how I should act a certain way, and my bad attitude, and blah, blah, blah... I just lost it. I was so tired of being singled out and hearing how bad I was. I thought, "What was I, her personal mission in life?" I felt so trapped. She came up to me and started shaking her finger at me. I stopped listening to what she was yelling about. She threatened to get the rubber hose and I just snapped. I started hitting her in the chest. I don't remember hitting her hard; I just wanted her to back off and leave me alone. (In trauma healing, I have learned that *'hurting people' hurt people.*)

Father heard the commotion and came in to put a stop to it.

He sent me to my room for a while and came in later to give me a licking. I had reached the point of not even caring if he beat or even killed me. "Go ahead pops; give me all you've got!" I said to myself. I was filled with such hatred towards Leslie and towards my own mother too.

After he spanked me and left my room, I remember thinking, "Father doesn't hit anything like mother does. That was nothing in comparison to her beatings." I truly believe he could have really hurt me if he wanted to, but he used restraint. He was pretty mad at me and I was grounded again to my room. That was the first and the last time I hit Leslie.

Years later my father told me that while I was growing up, I'd blow up about every six months and it took them a couple of weeks to get me settled back down. So I got to thinking "Could I have been the family pressure cooker?" With all of the hell and torment, we inflicted on each other within our secret walls at home. Maybe I just personalized and internalized it so much that every so often it became unbearable for me to continue stuffing it in.

Throughout this book, I have shared sayings my mother used to say. Now I'd like to tell you one of Leslie's favorite sayings,

"I know you like a book!" She always said to me. Oh man, I hated to hear those words with a passion! Of course, she'd say that whenever I tried to defend myself against something I'd done. Leslie always cut me off in midstream and say,

"Oh James, you think you're so smart. Well I know you like a book!"

So I'd love to find out if she really did, then ask her, why she wasn't more understanding, instead of condemning. Today though, if she were to ever read these pages, I can probably bet that she didn't even know the half..."

-CHAPTER TWENTY TWO-

"I'm a Financial Burden."

*A*t the end of my seventh grade year, the school nurse went through and checked everyone for scoliosis (Sway back). If the problem was caught early enough it could be corrected. It was determined that I had the beginning stages of Sherman's disease, (Hunchback). So I had to wear a back brace for a few years. I felt like a weirdo, which was the last thing a teenager wants. I was the only one in our whole school who had to wear this weird awkward contraption.

"Hey look, it's the hunchback of Aberdeen Junior High." Some kids teased.

Leslie took me out of school on the days that I had to visit my specialist. His office was in downtown Tacoma. I enjoyed those trips very much, because it was just her and I. We lived a distance from the city, so the trip was an all day affair, plus we got to stop somewhere for lunch. I felt special on those days, even though I dreaded the doctor's appointments.

My medical bills were an issue during those years. My parents fought constantly about how to juggle the payments. They often had to put off buying something they wanted in order to keep up with a particular payment. I felt it was my fault for all of the family's financial problems.

Even before the medical bills, my parents were in a habit of bringing up just how ungrateful I was. They'd buy me an article of clothing and or a toy, but then typically I would get in trouble a day or maybe even a week or two later for doing something wrong.

"We just bought you something and this is the thanks we get? I cannot believe how ungrateful you are. I have half a mind to take it away from you. You don't deserve anything!" They would inevitably say. It got to the point where every time they gave me something I was overwhelmed with anxiety. I thought to myself, "Uh, oh! Okay, Jimmy, you'd better be on your best behavior." I'd battle with myself, "You idiot, stay out of trouble. Just try to be good long enough until they forget they got you this present!" Then I would plead with myself, "Please do better this time. Please show them you appreciate their gift and that you're worthy of their love." I'd go back to my room, and sit quietly while I thought about what I really wanted to say to my father. "See, Father, I've been good. I always want to be good. I'm sorry I mess up sometimes. Daddy I love you, do you love me? Sure I like the present, but I really need to hear from you that you love me sometimes, that's all."

Even today, I never feel comfortable spending money on myself; I usually talk myself out of things. Because of my parents, fighting over money and me taking it personally, when I do finally buy myself something, it has to be a sale of the year. I'm a tightwad to this day, just ask anybody who knows me and they'd agree.

"Where Do I Belong?"

During my adolescent years there were many times when I felt like an outsider, especially when Leslie made it a point, to introduce Jason and I as her 'Husband's children'. Whenever she would take us kids anywhere and she would see an acquaintance that hadn't met us, they'd say,

"So these are your children?" Then, instead of just replying,

"Yes." and introduce us, she would always make a point to distinguish us by saying, "JR and Rachel are *my* children; and this is Jason and James, these are my husband's kids." Which was true, but I always felt sad about the way she had to make sure people knew we didn't come out of her womb; that we didn't belong to her.

While I was growing up, I'd always refer to her as my mom. It was only when I would be talking to my friends and they'd get confused and asks me.

"Now, are you talking about your real mom or your step-mom?" Only then would I make the distinction. Even now, writing this book I'm making a distinction between my two moms when normally I wouldn't.

I recall it was an age thing with her. Like she was trying to say, "I'm getting old, but I'm not old enough to have kids *that* age!" It seemed silly, really, because she was fifteen when she was pregnant with JR and I'm just a little over a year older than he is.

My father had his own way of inadvertently making me feel unworthy of living in the Petra home. From time to time during our family trips, we often passed a local detention center for boys. *Every* single time we passed it my father would say,

"You know, James, if you don't straighten up, in a couple of years you'll be old enough to be sent there." He'd threaten as we drove past it. He would tell me something like that whether I was presently in trouble or not. I'd think to myself, "Where the heck did that come from? What did I do to make him say that?" His comment would upset me so much that I rarely got any enjoyment from our trips. I'd just sit there through the day condemning myself and think, "Jimmy, you're bad. You're not wanted, and you're in the way. You're just an obligation."

"You live here because your mother got tired of raising you!" My father actually told me that once. Those words hurt me more than mother's worst beatings.

It got to the point where I'd try my very best to be extra good way before our trips. Then on that day, all the way there I'd pray, "Please make father not see the boys home. Please help me make my parents see I'm trying to be a good boy!" But no such luck.

"You know, James, you're old enough to be sent to that home. You keep messing up and that's where you'll end up." Father would inevitably say.

~

"Shame started out as a two-person experience, but as I got older I learned how to shame all by myself."

-CHAPTER TWENTY THREE-

Suicide Attempt Number One

I was thirteen the first time I tried to kill myself. I realize now that nobody knew I was suffering from depression including me. I remember a couple of months prior to that time; my grandmother, Leslie's mom, gave me a gift. She knew I was growing up and getting too big for toys, so she bought me a big gift package of men's 'British Sterling' hygiene and cologne products. It was a wonderful present, but I took it as she was telling me that I stunk and that perhaps I would get the hint with her present. Of course, that was the furthest thing from her intentions. However, at the time, I was so embarrassed and upset with her and myself that I thought, "Man, even grandma thinks I'm a piece of crap." Sadly, I didn't talk to her for almost a month. Finally, we got that misunderstanding ironed out. After that, it became the best gift ever.

I had been having a rough year. I was having a rotten life. I recall father making a comment to Leslie during one of my many turbulent episodes, saying, "Isn't it just typical of his mother. Mess him up during his childhood and then ship him to his father for his teen years to try and straighten the boy up!" I was in the same room when he told her that. He acted like I was invisible. I felt like a thorn in his side. What he said was true, but it hurt so much to hear it from my own father.

My self-destructive thoughts were taking their toll. "I'm a freak. Nobody wants me. I don't belong anywhere. I'm in the way and I'm a gross sinner. Why can't I control my sexual urges? Stupid Tallywacker, I cannot even stand myself! I'm causing all of this pain and problems within my family. Even JR told me that I'm not wanted here and that it was better before I started living with them.

I thought if I just killed myself then I wouldn't be a bother to anyone. Then they would all be happy. I wouldn't cost them any more money, time, or trouble!" I had serious suicidal thoughts for two weeks. Then one night I finally talked myself into taking a steak knife to bed with me. I laid there in bed and tried to stick it through the middle of my chest. However, I was only able to puncture the skin and then it hurt too much to press any harder, so I stopped.

I had gotten the idea of killing myself by stabbing a knife through the chest from watching someone do it on television. My failed attempt made me feel even more worthless because I couldn't even do *that* right!

-CHAPTER TWENTY FOUR-

"Who Cares?"

I majored in art and drama all through junior and high school. My art and drama instructors did wonders for my self-esteem. They saw my creative potential and continually praised and encouraged me to continue cultivating my talents. These educational mentors served as a lifeline throughout my tumultuous teenage years. I will always be grateful to them.

Most teachers probably do not realize just how much some students rely on them to fill the void in their desolate lives. Good teachers have a gift of giving, without expecting perfection in return. These kinds of teachers are sometimes lucky enough to have a pupil of theirs stop by years later to say,

"Thanks for caring. If it wasn't for you I wouldn't be here today." Someday I may cross paths with my former teachers and thank them for caring, because after my suicide attempt I just poured my heart and soul in to the arts.

In the book, 'The Resilient Self' childhood survivors express their intense grief through poetry. I wrote poems in my teen years. Many times, I used to show them to Leslie. One day she asked,

"Why is it that all your poems are so depressing and full of death? Can't you write some happier ones? You're bumming me out!" Of course, I took offense and stopped sharing any more poems with her, except for the happy poems I'd copy from other books. 'The Resilient Self' helped me to discover I was grieving my lost childhood and so desperately needed to talk to someone.

"Teachers of our children: *PLEASE* continue to show them

who cares.

You may just be saving a precious, fragile life."

-CHAPTER TWENTY FIVE-

Mother Reaps What She Sowed

Living in a rural part of Washington it was difficult for a teenager to get a real job if they didn't have their own car. Most kids in rural families worked at the orchards to help pay for school clothes and extra things they wanted.

In 1980, I turned sixteen; I really wanted to work at a real job making an hourly wage. I was old enough to get a job in town, but I didn't have a car, or the desire to learn how to drive one. So after talking with my parents, they decided to let me visit my mother in California for the summer and find a job where I could ride my bicycle to and from work.

It had been four years since I last lived with mother. Through those years, she had visited her family in Washington; it was only during those visits that I'd briefly see her. However, the thought of living under her roof again, even for three months, troubled me. But, my desire to work for good money outweighed my apprehensions. I thought, "Okay, I'm going to be on my very best behavior. I'm going to try so hard to be good and do everything right. I think I can even remember better now so that I will be able to do everything she tells me without her repeating herself. She'll be so proud of me!" At the same time, however, I remembered her extreme punishment. I didn't want to put up with that anymore. "I'm bigger now." I said to myself, "I'm not going to stand for her hitting me anymore. I shouldn't have to be so scared of her; she's my mother for crying out loud. Well, if she does hit me then I'm going to stand up to her and tell her how I really feel about that. But I won't be giving her a reason to hurt me, because I'm going to be the perfect gentleman she always wanted me to be."

Well, I got a job; washing dishes at a family-style restaurant, I rode my bike to and from work. I was on my best behavior all summer and I could tell my mother was trying her best, too. I almost made it through the whole visit without a confrontation. Almost being the key word. Just two weeks before I was to leave, Mother and I got into a heated debate. Neither one of us would back down. I was the cocky teenager who knew it all. We were face to face screaming at one another when suddenly she reaches up and slaps me in the face. By sheer reflex, I slapped her back before I'd even realized what I had done. By then it was too late. She was stunned and shocked. I just stood there in disbelief too, not to mention that I was scared to death. I saw her blinking a couple of times, trying to register what had just occurred. Mother and I both discovered that I was not her little boy anymore. She simply backed away and told me to go to my room and then she called my step-dad. When he got home, she told him *her* version of what happened. He came into my room and talked to me, he did all the talking. He wouldn't listen to me.

"Even *if* she did hit you first, she's your mother and you don't *ever* hit your mother!" He told me. So after the lecture I was grounded for the last two weeks of my stay. I never hit her again.

Ironically, Mother worked out of the home for a number of years after she shipped me up north to live with my father. She ran a licensed daycare center. When I was in my early twenty's, I got to pondering her little business choice and thought, "Who the heck reviews the qualifications of people that desire to care for other people's children? If they had interviewed her own kids, we would have had to cut a deal if they wanted the truth in exchange for being placed in the witness protection program." Mother actually did quite well, which reinforced my poor self-esteem. I rationalized that how she treated me was my fault. I was bad. I am a piece of crap.

That summer vacation was a real milestone for me. I had my first real job. But most important of all, as the years went by, I realized it would also be the last time my Mother ever laid a hand on me in anger.

-CHAPTER TWENTY SIX-

Hypocrites–So Many Masks

 $\mathcal{D}$ uring my senior year of high school, I began to think more about my future, not so much about my future education, but more about my survival. Where would I live? How would I support myself? I had yet to pick up any good vibes from my parents. They made comments like,

"We're not going to be like some parents who allow their children to stay at home and mooch off of them." Or, "You know you're old enough to be kicked out of this house if you don't start flying right!" It's a wonder I just didn't live out of a suitcase in anticipation of those words coming true.

I was also constantly concerned, frustrated, and angered by our so-called 'Christian Family Love.' With all the "What would Jesus do to you if he were here right now and saw what you have done?" Or, "What would Jesus think if he were your parent and you pulled something like that in front of him? Why he'd be embarrassed and ashamed of you, too!" Etc... Etc...

At our weekly bible meetings, we studied about family life. This information was needed very much in our household. Unfortunately, I learned early on that religion was just another mask to wear. Oh yes, the bible was drilled and lectured into our little minds, but rarely ever taught by example. We all had tons of bible knowledge, but once we got home and put up our bibles, we also put away our Religious Masks

What our rendition of quality family time together and what our studies encouraged were two different things. Our family night was every Monday night, and it consisted of watching television together as a family. Father would watch his Monday night football one week and then the next week we'd all watch 'Little House on the Prairie,' that show would get us all crying before the first commercial break. I was glad Laura Engalls finally grew into her teeth. It was many years later before I'd realize that Melissa Gilbert and I were the same age. I had hoped to be as old as the girl that played Mary, Laura's older sister, because I had such a crush on her back then.

I cherished those evenings together, but even though we were all in the same room, we didn't talk. Conversation was allowed only during the commercial breaks. I learned to hate television for stealing our family's time to communicate. Even if we didn't know how to communicate with each other properly, we could have learned. I despised the TV so much that when I moved out on my own, it was eight years before I bought one of my own.

Growing up in the Petra house there was rarely two weeks that would pass without hearing some kind of bickering and arguing. The atmosphere in the house was poisonous; voices' rising up to a hundred decibels was the norm. It wasn't easy growing up in World War III. I recall many times when my father and Leslie were literally at each other's throats, and suddenly the telephone would ring. Father would continue to yell and argue on the way to answer the phone, then at the last second, just before picking up the receiver, he had the uncanny ability change his tone to a loving, cheerful man of the house.

"Hello?" He'd answer with a big smile. "Well, how's it going? No, no, you didn't interrupt a thing. Sure, what can I do ya for?" He'd ask while grinning and showing nothing but his pearly white teeth. Man, he was good at wearing his mask.

Father worked in the timber industry for years until he hurt his knees, after that he worked in the Public Relations Department at the main office of the mill. He was a real natural at PR. He even won 'PR. Man of the Year' on many occasions. Later his health improved and he resumed his previous position on the line at the lumber mill where he made better money.

Leslie was not a happy person. Father always told us kids.

"Mom's on the rag twenty-eight days a month!" It really wasn't funny though, she did seem to have *pre*-PMS and *post*-PMS. Eventually, she had a Hysterectomy, but sadly, her moods didn't change much.

I recall one particularly heated fight between the two of them. It lasted for days. It finally ended with dads words,

"Look, woman, the *only* thing I expect from you is two things. One: I expect a hot meal ready for me when I get home, and Two: You give me sex when I want it. That's it! That's all you're good for to me. I don't expect you to do another damn thing." Then he huffed out of the house and headed for the wood shed to vent his anger by splitting fire wood.

My step-mother seemed utterly devastated by his hateful words. She was humiliated.

At the time I thought, "Wow! Dad finally got the last word! Boy, he finally put her in her place. Right on, Dad!" She went to her room and cried for a very, very long time. We walked around very softly that evening. The house was actually quiet for a change.

Nobody outside our family ever knew about the kind of war zone it was in our home. We all wore the "Everything's Just Fine"

Masks so well.

In my trauma healing, I've read a lot about how unresolved issues and toxic shame affects us and how we spread dysfunction and pain without even realizing it. I discovered that Leslie had her share of shame-based secrets—after I turned eighteen my older brother Jason and I visited our former foster mother. She told us things that helped us understand Leslie better.

You see Leslie was placed in foster care when she was an out of control fifteen year old that was pregnant, with JR, and had very poor self-esteem.

Jason and I were placed in the same foster home, when my dad come visit us he met Leslie and the rest is history. Looking back now, I can see that our step-mom tried miserably to cover over her own internal living hell with religion.

-CHAPTER TWENTY SEVEN-

A REAL Mask that Fits

My senior year at school was great because I was able to be the Elementary Art Instructor. Due to budget cuts, the school system could no longer afford to pay for an Art Teacher. So my high school Art teacher talked to the School Board about letting *me* instruct. The Board agreed to let me earn class credit for being a Student Art Instructor.

It was the best experience of my life. I went to my three regular senior classes in the morning, and then I'd walk the two miles to the elementary school during lunch. In the afternoon, I planned and taught art projects for grades 1 thru 6, six hundred and fifty students in all.

Before the school year ended, I was also able to put my drama skills to use. I worked up a one-man theatrical show for the children. I performed several Pantomime skits, complete with costume and make-up. The kid's loved it and the teachers were amazed. After each performance, with all of the applause and praise, "This mask is wonderful! I know how to wear *this* one well. I felt safe, people were smiling, and smiles are safe." I said to myself, as I took a bow and thanked them for allowing me to entertain them. I began to realize that I was hooked on acting.

-CHAPTER TWENTY EIGHT-

Leaving the Nest and Free at Last

My graduation day was a very emotional time for me. After the ceremony, my parents gave me a little party and had some of the friends over.

All through graduation night, I was having a hard time with my 'Happy Time' mask. Even my father noticed. He had pulled me aside and gave me two hundred dollars and said to me,

"I love you, son." I thought to myself. "That's nice pops, but you're a little late don't you think?" I responded by saying,

"Thanks, dad, I love you too so very much." Then he hugged me and as he did I was thinking, "This is different. I could sure get used to this." Man, I had needed that hug and I needed to hear those words a long time ago, and what about the hugging, how hard was it to hug your own flesh and blood anyway? My emotions were running wild. After we hugged, I told him,

"Thanks dad. Thanks for the party and thanks for the money." I can honestly say that he was a very good provider when it came to material things. We didn't have an excess, but we never did without, I would have given my eyeteeth to hear these words of love and affection from any one of my dysfunctional parents:

"James, I want you to know something.
No matter what you do in life,
I am always going to love you.
You can be honest with me and tell me the truth.
I may not approve of everything you do,
but I'm always going to love you."

Earlier that day I had taken on the task of packing up all my belongings. It was difficult to know what to take and what to leave behind. A friend from school helped me move out that very night. As my friend and I drove away that evening, I was an emotional wreck. I cried for a whole two weeks after leaving home.

I now realize what a struggle it was to wear all of those dysfunctional Masks, which I had been exposed to through the years. Some Masks did not fit me well, like the 'Happy Time' mask, and the 'I've Got Everything under Control' mask. The 'Petra Pride' mask was just too heavy. I wasn't very good at wearing it. It seemed like I always found a way to embarrass my family and myself. I was forever getting the look that said, "Can't you just get it together, damn it!" However, my parents made sure I never took off one mask. It was the mask of 'Family Secrets,' it weighed heavily on my shoulders, that's why I had trouble wearing all the other ones. This mask carried cancerous secrets from the Petra's, and my mother, Mr. Gomez, Gamin the sixth grader, and Uncle Everett, along with my own toxic shameful secrets.

I moved out and got a job washing dishes at a nice family restaurant. After the grieving phase of leaving the nest, I started to feel free. My goodness, I had freedom and I didn't know what to do with myself.

I started hanging out with one of the cooks at work. His name was Marty.

He was about ten years older than I was, and he was great fun. He was so full of life, laughs and ------liquor. We worked the graveyard shift and Marty would talk a waitress into going with us to get some beer at 7:30 am, then we would wait until 10:00 am for the bars to open up and we would go bar hopping. I felt so lost and lonely. Marty tried to help me forget my troubles. While he drank like a fish, I would sit there and nurse my glass of beer, trying to look twenty-one, but nervous and probably looking out of place. I saw a couple of bartenders look suspiciously towards my direction, but neither said anything. I tried to act as if I was having a great time. I wore my 'Happy Time' mask, but inside I felt very empty. We went bar hopping a total of three times and to a champagne brunch once. I was drunk only twice in that two-month excursion. I'm such a cheap drunk, it took all of four beers to get me toasted and it didn't make me dance around with a lamp shade on my head like they do in the movies, it just made me real sleepy. I didn't even wake up with a headache or anything. Sarcastically, I thought, "Boy that was fun. Far out! Yeah, right!" That was the extent of my wild days. It didn't take me long to realize that those people were in the fast lane going nowhere in life.

Even through my adult years, I've been too cheap to waste my money on such an expensive addiction. When I go out on the town with friends, I'm the official designated driver. I feel very proud of myself for that. Always the caretaker or maybe it makes me feel like I'm in control of not only of myself, but over other people too.

Grandpa Dies

Within a month of my heart wrenching tumultuous exit from home, my Grandpa Petra, who had only been retired for two years, passed away from a massive heart attack.

I was not at all ready to face my family yet. My soul was still mending. I was desperately attempting to make sense of my life. Wondering where exactly I stood with my father and step-mom. I was so angry, hurt, and confused that I had decided I just couldn't pretend to be a proud member of the Petra clan and attend my grandfather's funeral. This was a decision I would regret down to this day. Although no one ever said anything about my absence, I lived with my own demons named Shoulda, Woulda and Coulda.

I should have been there for my father. Bottom line was, though, I just didn't feel worthy of being around such "greatness" anymore. That constant cloud of depression loomed above, and I just couldn't push my own personal problems aside.

-CHAPTER TWENTY NINE-

Making Money off the Mask

While I was working at the restaurant, I became friends with one of the regular customers. One day we got to talking about our different talents and found out, we had some in common. I told him about my love for acting and performing pantomime. He told me that he had a clown get-up and did children parties for his friends and family. We decided to become business partners. We called ourselves 'Mimes & Clowns.' We did quite well for a part-time side job. Our very first job was at a stationary store where we bartered for a set of business cards in exchange for our promoting their grand opening. I continued to do grand openings and special sales weekends for businesses, and he did birthday parties. I even traveled to Sacramento, California and entertained one week at a Macy's in California, also we performed at the Washington State Fair. We even made the front page of the Seattle Post.

It was a lot of hard work, but I felt rewarded for my efforts and the money was good but the smiles were great. They always made me feel safe. I made people happy and that was good. I felt accepted and I was being praised. I felt needed and loved. But, then I started to think that that was the only way I could be accepted. I thought I needed to be the life of the party, even without the makeup, even without a party. I was always witty, fun, and sarcastic. That was how I stayed in control.

Since those days, I'm very proud to say that I've entertained people from coast to coast and for audiences of more than a thousand people at one time. I felt blessed to have stumbled onto something I could do that made people laugh. Forget about their pain and troubles, and my own pain, even if for just a moment.

I was comfortable wearing a real mask. I could be anybody I wanted to be. Finally, I began to understand what my family was so good at; but I asked myself, "Why do I feel the need to hide behind the makeup to 'Perform' for people?" Even with my newfound freedom of being on my own and having my own business, I continued wearing the many Petra Masks. I found myself on top of my little world feeling lonely and scared to death. I was afraid that I wouldn't be accepted for just being myself. I'd been hiding for so long; even I didn't know who I truly was. There were too many secrets, too much shame, and *Too Many Masks*.

-CHAPTER THIRTY-

My First Kiss

My first kiss was with a girl named Ronda. She was seventeen, a year younger than I was, and she was my first girlfriend since Cassy broke my heart back in the seventh grade.

After I moved out on my own, I started to visit her on my days off. It soon turned into a budding romance. One afternoon, we went to see the movie 'On Golden Pond'. I decided before hand that I was going to ask her to kiss me. Thankfully, she agreed, but only if it was during the movie where it was dark and nobody would see us.

I was eighteen years old and it was going to be the first time I'd ever kissed a girl. Needless to say, I remembered nothing of the movie. I was so nervous, and when we actually did kiss, I was thinking, "Oh gosh, I hope my parents didn't follow us to the movie house. Man, this is great! Oops, I hurt my lip with her teeth." I had such an erection that I wet myself. We kissed about three more times before the movie ended. I must have been doing it right, because she wasn't complaining. As we left the theater, I couldn't help but think and feel like I had just had sex with Ronda. I thought everyone could tell we had been kissing. I felt so embarrassed. As we walked back to her house arm in arm, she asked,

"How did you like kissing me?"

"Great, great, it was wonderful. You okay?" I asked. "Yeah great, I'm fine too." I said as I secretly nursed my split lip.

Ronda and I eventually mastered kissing and moved on to making out. She was the girl of my dreams, and we were going to get married. I bought her a wedding ring set, the kind with one of those microscopic diamonds chips. She and I were engaged then broke up in about a six-month period; her father stepped in and put a stop to it. He said that we were too young and not ready for marriage. I was devastated and angry with him at first. I said to myself, "He just doesn't understand. We love each other. We can get through anything with enough love. Didn't he believe in the words to that old Sonny and Cher song, 'I Got You Babe', didn't he know anything?"

I was utterly crushed. I was so desperate to be in a loving relationship. I just needed to belong somewhere and to somebody. However, after the depression subsided from our break up, I had to admit that we were too young. We were making out more than making mature plans for our future. I found myself alone and abandoned again.

-CHAPTER THIRTY ONE-

Meeting My Trophy Wife

I met Alison while doing volunteer work before I moved to the east coast. It was in the dead of winter with snow on the ground at 6:30 in the morning when we crossed paths. As I approached her, I thought, "My goodness, she is the most beautiful woman I had ever seen in my entire life!" Even though she was bundled up, her auburn red, hair flowed gracefully down over her petite shoulders, with the brightest hazel green eyes. Incidentally, by then my own hair had finally gone back to its natural color.

She was about 5'3" in height and very sweet. I was smitten. After I rolled my tongue back into my mouth, I introduced myself. As I poured on the charm, we walked down the street for a much-needed coffee break; we finally exchanged phone numbers as we left the café, and went our separate ways. About two weeks later, we went roller-skating with a group of friends. All the while, I kept thinking, Alison seems she's so spiritual minded. Leslie would be happy. On top of that, she is extremely pretty. She'd be a real showpiece. My family would be so proud.

Advice from a Friend Goes Unheeded

Paul was a dear friend. He was a couple years older than I

was and I truly valued his opinion. We talked once a month. Well, after eight months of observing Alison, my friend had some difficult advice for me. One day we were on the phone and he said,

"Jimbo, I don't want to hurt your feelings, but your girlfriend is a complete airhead. Seriously, she has no horse sense. Alison is not right for you. I know you pretty well and I know it's not a good match. Her mother does the decision making for her. EVERYTHING! Yeah, she loves God, but she's about as bright as a total eclipse." Then he concluded,

"Jimbo, as your friend, I just felt I needed to tell you before your heart got too involved." But, it was already too late. I was in too deep.

"I'll help her then." I said in reply. "I can do that. Her mother is just too overbearing. It'll be fine. I just love her so I can…" I started believing the Masks I wore were real. I began to think I finally had it all together and that I was in control.

After hanging up and turning a deaf ear to my best friend, I continued to reason with myself, "I can mold Alie and teach her how to be her own person. She's an airhead, great, so I have an empty slate to work with. No problem, I can handle this. Alie is sooo beautiful and she loves God, and she loves me. What more can I ask for, I am blessed!" Man, my heart, and hormones were so far gone. I was like a mule with blinders on in a mule train.

The Start of Our Regrets

A year later, I decided to propose to Alison. Since I had given my friend, Paul the wedding set that Ronda gave back to me. He asked,

"Jimbo do you want those rings back so you can give them to Alison?"

"No way!" I told him, and then I thought about it and said, "Well, wait a minute… No, that would be so wrong and besides I bought Alie a ring when I visited New York one four-day weekend."

"Yeah, from a pawn shop for thirty-five dollars!" He said smugly.

"Okay yes, you're right. But, it's from *New York City*." I retorted.

Unfortunately, it wasn't long before I found out that my best friend was telling the truth about my fiancée and her mother. Rosemary was a very controlling person and Alison did not have an opinion or a thought of her own. She let everyone around her especially her mother influence her.

I really resented Rosemary's eagle claws. Rosemary was smart enough to see through my facade. She knew I didn't know what I was doing or talking about half the time and she called me on it every chance she could. Alison did her best to stand up for me. Sadly, one of the big reasons she wanted to marry me was to get away from her mother's control.

Rosemary and Alison's father divorced many years ago, leaving Rosemary to raise Alison by herself. She eventually married another 'loser of a drunk', as she called him, and had another child, this time she had a boy, named Andy. Rosemary finally wised up and left him. She took care of her children the best that she could.

Alison once said that before they found God, her mother was a real motorcycle mama. Almost all of her family was heavily into drugs and parties. My fiancée said it was a real blessing that she and her mother had cleaned up their lives. Alison told me that she had, 'slept with hundreds of guys before she turned her life around'. The first time she told me that I replied,

"I don't mind, the past is the past!" Then I told myself, "Heck, I wasn't worthy of marrying a virgin anyways, even though I had never been with a woman."

Regrettably, one-time just weeks before our wedding day, I

went to visit Alison where she was a live in hospice care provider. I arrived as usual and pulled up a chair alongside the bedridden man Alison took care of. He had the TV volume cranked up high, enjoying his daily dose of 'Perry Mason' reruns.

"James, I want to show you something. Something you'll be getting after our wedding." She said as she left the room.

"Okay." I said. I had no idea what she had in mind. I knew she kept all of her wedding shower gifts in her room. Then after a few minutes, Alison told me to come into her room, and there she stood-----Totally naked! I was absolutely shocked. As she continued to stand there modeling for me, I thought, "What possessed her to do this? Nice butt. Has she lost her mind completely?!?"

"So" She said in a sexy voice, "What do you think?"

"Nice, rr-really nice. Great Alie, great, thanks for the peek." I replied as I left and returned to the living room, stunned and in total disbelief. I sat there dazed for a long time. I kept asking myself, "Did that really happen? Tell me that did not just happen?" I paused and thought, "Well, so much for that perfect and pure courtship we were supposed to have."

Even though nothing happened further, I still felt so dirty and ashamed. I was ashamed of myself and of her. That incident would prove to be the first of many regrets throughout our relationship.

-CHAPTER THIRTY TWO-

My Wedding Day Blues

Everything went fine on our wedding day. It was a beautiful, yet modest affair. During the ceremony, Alison looked like she had just walked off the front page of a bridal magazine. She was gorgeous. I kept admiring how beautiful she looked in white. My mind began to race, "Why is she in white? Why am I in white? I should be wearing bright neon sinner red!" I felt like a fake. I was so nervous my 'Happy Time' mask slipped a little, but I caught it as I continued to talk to myself, "Jimbo, what have you gotten yourself into? Oh yeah, sex tonight. Man, I'm going to be sick. Why are we in white? Oh that's right, the show. It's our wedding, this is what I'm supposed to do, and everyone approves.

My mother made the trip from California. She looks pretty. Oh look, she colored her hair and it's almost the same color mine is. Wow, she looks younger. I'm the first of her four children to get married. I guess she's feeling old. My father and Leslie are sitting there proud and smiling. Oh, yeah, keep smiling, all smiles. Oops, my mask slipped again."

Thinking back on our wedding night now, some sayings come to mind like; "The anticipation is greater than the end reward." And or, "Hope is better than the having." I tried so hard to be a manly twenty one year old, but I didn't have a clue how to interact with my new bride and to pull it off like they do in the movies. I finally told Alison my true feelings.

"That's okay Jimmy." She said, "Don't you worry; I'll teach you everything you need to know."

"Okay, great!" I replied. However, when she told me that, I just thought, "Was that supposed to reassure and comfort me?" I felt even more embarrassed than before. I felt powerless and so unmanly. I just bowed my head and prayed for the lights to go out. I felt like that little 6 year old from years earlier, sitting in the front yard with only a cloth diaper on and people laughing at me.

While we were making love, I couldn't help but worry that possibly any second my father and or Leslie was going to burst through the door of our suite and catch us, then condemn us to death and damnation. I kept battling with myself, "I'm married. We're married and this is all right. It's okay. I have a piece of paper to prove we're married. They were at the wedding, stupid. Okay, everything's fine." Afterwards, she asked me,

"Well, what do you think?" I thought, "Oh, its evaluation time?" However, I replied,

"Great, great super. Yeah it, it was all I've ever thought it would be." Then I asked,

"Was it good for you, Alie? Yeah? Good yeah, me too, me too." Then she said, "It gets better over time and practice." I thought, "I sure hope so." But said,

"That's wonderful. I can't wait. Well, goodnight."

It took me almost three months to get over my paralyzing fear of being caught having sex with my wife. I just kept having these visions of my parents busting down the door and saying,

"What in God's name do you think you're doing young man? Can't you keep your penis in your pants for five minutes? You are such an embarrassment to this family. That's it, come on and get dressed. You're going to the boy's home for sure this time, buster!" I finally hung our marriage certificate right outside our bedroom door, just in case they did show up and forget they were at our wedding.

I don't have to explain how that fear really messed up my performance in bed. But, God love her, Alison did teach me everything she knew, such the pro as she was. I couldn't help but remember her comment to me about teaching me everything I needed to know, our first night together. I wanted to ask her, "Do you take checks? Cause, I'm a little low on cash right now!" I resented her statement about that. I continued to feel weak and vulnerable. Every so often throughout our marriage, she mentioned the "hundreds and hundreds, probably close to a thousand guys" she had slept with before she was seventeen. I despised her for making those comments, but each time I replied,

"Well, you know that's okay. You're the best woman I've ever had." All the while, I'd smile and try to convince myself that her words didn't hurt me.

Tough Transitions

It didn't take long before the honeymoon phase was over. Rosemary still had such a tight grip on Alison. Like a tightly bound spring. It reminded me of a statement I read in the book 'When Acceptance Is Denial': "Once you have obliterated a person intellectually, sexually, spiritually and emotionally, they'll never want to make a decision again. They will instead look for safety in having someone else decide for them." Finally, Rosemary reluctantly handed the reins over to me. There I was, holding that massive responsibility with both hands, so-to-speak, and thinking, "I can handle this, no problem." But also "What the heck have I gotten myself into?" Then back to, "No problem, everything is under control. Yes, everything's fine." Unfortunately, for Alison, I never learned the difference between holding her hand and chaining her soul.

The transition from single life to married life was tough. It doesn't come with a foolproof manual. Even if it did, I wouldn't have read it, because I thought that I had it all together. I was "God!" and Alie, well Alison, was such an embarrassment to me. Whenever she would say or do something that I thought was stupid, I'd just cringe especially if we were around our friends. I'd think, "Oh, man, did she just say that? People are laughing and they're looking at me as if to say, 'Hey, Jimbo, you've got yourself a real bright one, don't ya?' This is so incredibly humiliating. Alison doesn't even know she's stupid. Okay, I'll lecture her again when we leave. Man! This job of training her sure is tough."

We usually ended up fighting all the way home, only later to have make-up sex. It's true what they say, "Make-up sex is *great*!"

Alison in Wonderland

One payday Alison met me at work for lunch. She had brought sandwiches from home and as we ate, we discussed our plans for the evening. I asked her,

"What would you like to eat for dinner?"

"I don't know."

"Well, what have you been craving, Mexican, Italian, or Chinese?"

"I don't know."

"Okay, do you have a favorite place to go and eat?"

"No, not really." I couldn't believe her responses. I was getting frustrated and thinking, "I'm trying to please my wife by letting her choose tonight's activities, and I'm coming up empty handed. Marriage is supposed to be a mutually deciding experience, a democracy at best. That darn mother-in-law and her totalitarian rulership!"

As I went back to work, I told her,

"Okay, Alie, I'll see you back here after work. Please be sure to be back before 4:00 pm so we can go to the bank and then go eat, and please think about where you want to eat."

I got off work at 4:00 pm and went out to the parking lot. To my surprise, I noticed that the car was in the same place. It had not been moved. Alison was sitting in the driver's seat just so happy and content. I asked her,

"Hey there, is something wrong with the car?"

"No." She replied as she slid over to the passenger side.

"You mean you've been sitting here since lunch?"

"Yup."

"What have you been doing?"

"Nothing."

"Nothing? What? Did you do any reading or anything?"

"No."

"Well, what were you thinking about for four hours?"

"Nothing." She said. I couldn't believe her. That was insane. I thought, "How can anyone just sit four hours and not do or read or think of *anything*? She has to be lying. Nobody is that brain dead!"

So I started the car and headed out for an evening on the town. I had to choose where to eat because she never did think of a place herself.

I eventually came to learn that if she did something similar to what she did that day, and she told me she wasn't thinking of anything, well, I'd believe she did just that.

~

~Love gone wrong also turns into dependency~

-CHAPTER THIRTY THREE-

"Our Fights Escalate, Wouldn't Father Be Proud?"

*T*wo months after we were married, I moved us out to the country. Back to the same area, I grew up in. I wanted to live a little closer to my father and definitely further away from my mother-in-law who lived in the city.

Alison and I continued to fight more and more, with each blow up getting worse than the last. Bickering and arguing with our voices raising higher,

"You're supposed to respect my headship!" I'd yell.

"You're supposed to take the lead in showing respect!" She spat back.

"What I say goes. I'm the man of this house. You obey me!" We went back and forth, louder, and louder.

Since I've been involved in my healing process, I have learned that, "People with the least self-control are the most controlling people."

Then, one day, when payday came around, Alison went out and spent her entire paycheck on crap for the cabin we were renting, and things for herself. I totally freaked out, because I was depending on both of our incomes to pay the bills.

"I'm the man of the house. I take care of the money here. You're too stupid to do it!" I snapped. I imagined that she had spent her paycheck just to spite me, but of course, she hadn't. I figured out later, she just wasn't thinking—again. But, at the time, I was livid. Then after three hours of fighting, she agreed to return most of the stuff. We made up, and then had great make-up sex, which sadly, that happened more often than just plain old happily married sex.

"Our Fights Escalate, Wouldn't Mother Be Proud?"

By the time I became an adult, I had an absolute abhorrence of animals. While growing up, JR my stepbrother just *had* to watch *every* Animal Kingdom show over and over again. I had thought that God had created enough different animals that one would be hard pressed to see a repeat. I grew so tired of watching those programs. "Darn them 'Mutual of Omaha' people. I would love to give our television 'A Piece of The Rock' right now!" I said to myself.

JR had so many fish tanks in his room. Each one filled with a different kind of critter. Our parents were always getting after him to clean his cages. A person could pass out from the smell just walking by his bedroom door.

One time, his pet snake escaped to roam around the house. It took him a while to find it before his mom did. Then a couple of days later, Leslie ran across about a dozen baby snakes in the living room while she was cleaning. She came unglued, and that was the last time snakes were allowed in the house.

After living with JR's obsession with animals, by the time I left the nest, I had developed quite a loathing for *any* kind of animal.

Before Alison and I were married, I made it absolutely clear that there would *not* be animals in our house.

"Okay, that's fine with me. Whatever you want, I'll just keep my dog at my mom's house. She doesn't mind taking care of him." She told me. Both Alison and her mother had those yippee, ankle biting, miniature poodles for pets. So I was quite surprised when I got home from work one Friday afternoon, not long after the paycheck incident, and heard the ear piercing barking from a pee-puddle-making, four-legged creature.

I stormed into the house and yelled over the barking,

"What in the Hell do you think you're trying to pull woman?" I was livid. As Alison scurried to pick up her dog and put it in the bathroom, she tried to reason with me, but I was a brick wall. We fought late into the evening. We were screaming back and forth, neither one willing to give an inch. At one point, we were face to face and I grabbed her to try to shake some sense into her. I told her,

"I'm the man of this house, damn it!" I don't know why I thought I had to keep reminding her about that. It never did seem to matter and I never got anywhere by saying it. She freed herself from my grip and she spat back.

"Don't you use that kind of language in this home!"

"It's my damn house, and I'll use any..." We were nose to nose once again and both just so fed up with each other's crap and Alison gets in my space like she was daring me, and I snapped. Before I realized what I was doing, I saw myself stepping down on her foot and at the same time I pushed her backwards, which made her lose her balance and go tumbling back over the furniture. I said to myself, "That will teach you, Bitch!" as I stormed into the kitchen to get a butcher knife. All the while I was thinking, "I'll show her whose boss of this house. I'm God, can't she get that through her stupid, empty, little red head?" I took the dog from the bathroom and headed for the front porch. In the back of my mind I thought, "Thank God we live way out in the country where no one's around." Alison ran after me.

"What are you going to do James?" she asked with her hazel green eyes in disbelief. I said to myself, "Good, I've finally got your attention. I'm through yelling and screaming. Nothing seemed to be working until now." I grabbed the creature around its neck and pinned it down on the porch. He scared to death and wet himself. I thought, "Oh, finally, shut your mouth too? Ain't that sweet. I had such power and control. I've got everyone's attention now, don't I?" Then in a low voice, I slowly and deliberately told Alison,

"Now, you *will* take this knife and you *will* kill this damn mutt. Because, there will be no animals living under my roof. Now, you can have this stuffed if you want, but under no circumstances will you be allowed to keep this dog here and it stay alive!" I was on a roll and I continued, "But why, you ask? Because you can't seem to take care of me very well, and I'll be damned if I let something else take up your time and devotion to distract you from this piss-poor job you're doing now. So I want you to take this knife right now and deal with it." Sadly, it boiled down to being all about me. I was God. Suddenly, Alison became what I had wanted her to become in the first place obedient and understanding. She was crying hysterically as she backed down from our fighting.

"Okay, okay, please don't make me kill him please. I'll take him back to moms in the morning. Okay, please?" She begged. I relaxed a little, as I said to her under my breath.

"That's better." I said as I released my death grip on the poor dog and it ran to his savior. I stood up, puffed out my chest, and walked tall, as I returned the butcher knife to the kitchen. Silence filled the house for the first time that evening. I fixed myself something to eat while Alison calmed her dog down and put it in the car for the night. She came in and apologized again for being out of line. I had calmed down, too. I was also sorry and I told her so. Soon after that, we were back to make-up sex, both of us were drained emotionally and physically. Before long, we fell fast asleep.

The next morning, Alison got up, and said she was on her way to take her dog back to her mother's and that she'd be back as soon as she could. Rosemary lived in Gig Harbor, which was an hour away. Before she left, I told her,

"Alie, honey, I'm sorry again for getting so mad last night. I'm so sorry I hurt you, too. I'm sorry, I didn't mean to."

"That's okay, sweetheart." She replied, "I should have listened to you. It was my fault too, for bringing the dog home. I'm sorry." We kissed and she was gone, and she stayed gone too! It took me three weeks of pouring on the ol' Jimmy charm to woo her back home.

When I found out that Alison had told her mother what had happened, I didn't care. But, when she told my parents, I thought, "Uh Oh, this ain't so good!" I tried to explain things to my father.

"Dad, you don't understand. You know she's an airhead. Remember, you've said so yourself? I know I got a little carried away. I shouldn't have hurt her; but Dad she just doesn't listen to me..." My father was just as upset as Rosemary was, and rightly so. All of our friends would eventually find out through the grapevine what I'd done to my wife. That left me feeling humiliated and utterly devastated. I pitied myself, nobody seems to understand or care what I have to deal with. "God, it's that woman you gave me! She just won't respect me and my headship, the bitch."

Alison and I finally reconciled. I agreed to go to a few anger management classes, but I still wasn't taking full responsibility and I was really ticked off at $65.00 a session I had to pay. So I put my 'Repentant' mask on and eventually worked my way back to good graces with the family and all was well. I just began to play it safer after that. I eased up on the physical abuse. I was still a control freak, and it was still her fault. But to some degree, I was willing to try to make some changes in our relationship. Alison had found a stray kitten and I let her keep it. I thought to myself, "See, look at me, I'm compromising. That was big of me, but I'm still the man!"

Sadly, when my anger problem was exposed my cherished friendship with Paul started to strain. Even after our marriage began to improve, my relationship with Paul would never be the same. He was the best man at our wedding and I was his when he got married. I cringe remembering how full of myself and immature I acted at his wedding. I was an embarrassment even to myself.

Through my experience, I have learned that it is difficult for friendships to survive when one person is judgmental and the other is self-condemning. However, I believe true friends can stand the test of time, through happy and sad tears, and then back to happy ones. Regrettably, neither Paul nor I were at that point yet.

Mother Always Said, "God Helps Those Who Help Themselves"

Even though our marriage was on the mend, there were still many times Alison seemed to test what I learned at those six Anger Management Classes. Many times, I'd come home from work tired and hungry, the same time every day and yet Alison never had dinner ready, not even started. Instead, my lovely wife was parked in front of the television watching 'Oprah', engrossed and holding on to her every word. I was fuming and thinking, "That darn feminist has wreaked havoc on our marriage more than once. She keeps pollutin' my Alie, telling her to 'Stand up to your mate. You have rights!' Oh, No! That TV set has got to go!" Bewildered I'd ask,

"Uh honey, where's supper?"

"Oh, I ate a sandwich when I got home. You hungry?" She asked without taking her eyes off 'Oprah'. I was so miffed at her lack of consideration. I thought, "Man, she is so selfish. Alison doesn't love me. If she did then she'd have dinner ready when I got home, like mom does when father walks through the door. How dare her treat me this way!" So it was off to the fights again that evening. After a few weeks of that, I tried to remind myself of what I'd learned from my Anger Management Classes: "Never expect something to be done for you. You can ask for it, but don't expect it. If you do, and it's not done, you get angry. But, if you ask without having such great expectations, then when something is done for you, all is well."

I also recalled what mother always used to say,

"God helps those who help themselves." So I just learned to save enough energy to cook when I got home.

-CHAPTER THIRTY FOUR-

Tragedy Strikes, "Where's My Family?"

*A*lison got pregnant within the first seven months of our wedding day. I could think of three main reasons she became pregnant, 1) too much make-up sex. 2) I knew enough about her before we married to not trust her memory to be responsible for taking birth control pills. 3) I didn't know enough about sex education and the proper use of condoms. I learned too late that you're not even supposed to penetrate during foreplay without protection.

I was horrified when she first told me. I thought, "We're not ready for this responsibility. We're not very good at being husband and wife, let alone Daddy and Mommy." I was just sick, but whom could I be mad at, just me, and that's no fun. It took awhile to accept my new role as 'father-to-be.'

Alison was in her fifth month of pregnancy when we were at a friend's house one early evening. They had some horses and Alison wanted to ride one before it got too dark. She loved horses, but being from the city she rarely got the chance to ride. I was concerned about her riding because she was inexperienced and pregnant. But, we discussed the subject at length and being the new loving husband that I was trying to be, I finally agreed and let her take a short trip around the barn.

Well, it was nearly dusk and the sunset was casting shadows off the weeds and stumps. Suddenly, something spooked the horse and it reared up into the air just like Silver does with the Lone Ranger. Only he wasn't in the saddle, my pregnant wife was. She fell straight back and landed on her butt with a thud. We all rushed to her side in a flash. Our friend and I helped her to the house and called her doctor. He said to keep her down and to bring her in if she started bleeding. So we went home and I played nursemaid.

In the last couple of months, I had finally come around to the idea that if I tried hard enough, I just might make a halfway decent father. So as I was taking care of Alie, I thought to myself, "I really do love my wife, I sure hope she and the baby are fine. I think I can handle taking care of our new addition. I know life has been tough on us, but we have both been trying so hard to be respectful and loving towards each other lately. I know we can put it all behind us and move on.

Won't my parents be proud of me when I show them I can be a good father? Surely, they will have to accept their new grandbaby. Then they'll have to accept me too!"

However, a week later she started spotting. We found out that the fetus had stopped growing soon after the fall. I rushed her to the hospital in McCleary and into the emergency room where they did an immediate D.N.C. I called Alison's mother who lived an hour away, and she came as soon as she hung up the phone. Then I called my father and Leslie they only lived thirty minutes away. I told them where we were and that Alison was losing the baby. Leslie answered the phone and said,

"Well, that's really sad to hear. What was she doing on a horse, anyhow? Well, I guess there's not much we can do now. Accidents happen. Um… is there… is there anything you want your father or I to do for you guys?" She asked. I paused for a long time, stunned at the indifference in her voice. Then I felt embarrassed that I called and disturbed them. I replied,

"No... No, there's nothing you guys can do. I just thought, I just thought...I'd call and let you know what's happening, that's all. I'm sorry."

"I'm sorry too, James." She said, "If you need anything be sure to call." That was the standard Petra response at the end of every conversation. I was under the impression that families should pull together during a crisis, leaving any differences behind to band together and support one another. I was devastated by her response. As I crumbled to my knees, I prayed that what was happening was just a sick dream.

Thank goodness, I called Paul before we headed for the hospital. He lived a few blocks away from the hospital and waited for us to arrive. Paul helped me to the waiting room and attempted to calm me down. Alison's mother finally showed up and added her support. By then our relationship was on the mend too. I found out who my real family was that day.

After Alison, was out of danger, I took her home. We grieved for quite awhile after losing the baby. We never asked if it was a boy or a girl. We decided to wait awhile before we 'planned' to have another one. She started taking 'the pill' for birth control and it was my job to ask her each night if she remembered to take it.

I gradually went through a grieving process over my relationship with my parents. I felt so hurt and bitterly angry with my parents over their lack of concern during our crises. After awhile I began to rationalize and justify their response thinking, "Maybe my father was just getting back at me for missing my Grandpa's funeral. Yeah, that's it. I knew it was my fault." Then I started to feel guilty about getting mad at them and instead I got angry with myself for being so selfish back about the funeral. I condemned myself all over again as I had done for years. "You know it's your own fault that you're an outcast. You are a freak and you deserve every bad thing that comes your way." My mother's words came back to haunt me. "You think you're so special! Poor little Jimmy, you think you're so abused! You little shit, stupid blockhead! You remember, you weren't even supposed to have been born either!" Yeah, I am pond scum, wicked, worthless, and a sinner.

-CHAPTER THIRTY FIVE-

A Career Choice that was Tailor Made

As I was growing up, I remember those adults who knew nothing about interacting with kids and yet felt obliged to try. They always asked that age-old question:

"What do you want to be when you grow up?" Heck, I wanted to be Gilligan on my own little Island with a Willy Wonka Factory. Boy, then I'd be set.

"What do I want to be? Well, um, dah, um, I want to be..." As I was talking, I thought to myself, "I want to be alive first of all. I'd just like to survive my childhood!" But instead, I'd say,

"I want to be a Fireman. Yeah that's it."

"Well isn't that sweet" They'd reply, "That's very noble of you."

But, if we had all became what we wanted to be back then, the world would be full of nothing but Policemen, Doctors, Teachers and of course, Firemen.

So when I turned twenty-two, I landed a job working for a company doing drywall, tape and texturing and painting. That would be my career trade. I chose a line of work that I found, I was a real natural doing it. I could cover over anything and make it appear fresh, clean, and new. Someday I may even be brave enough to have a slogan written across my work vehicle. Something like,

'Thou can cover over a multitude of sins. Painting and Faux Finishes'.

Working meant everything to the Petra family. I love to work. Most of us kids have become serious workaholics just like our father. I felt that people measured my worth and success by my accomplishments not just for being me. However, since I've been involved in my trauma healing I've learned, like all other '_____aholics', being a workaholic is an imbalance of priorities and values. It too, is a sickness.

-CHAPTER THIRTY SIX-

"If You Don't Acknowledge a Problem, Then It Simply Does Not Exist."
* Dave Pelzer

Like most married couples, Alison and I had been sharing intimate details of our lives while growing up. I really loved to communicate and gut talk. I felt blessed to be able to share my deepest thoughts and fears with someone finally. I had always envisioned that was part of what marriage was all about, being a friend for life.

One night, I went into detail with my wife about what Mr. Gomez and Uncle Everett had done to me. Alison listened with kind eyes and made me feel safe. She suggested that I tell my mother too. Alison told me that she was able to share things about her childhood with her own mother and that the sharing had brought them closer together.

Soon after that conversation, my mother came up from California and stayed with us while she attended her twenty-five year class reunion. They made her an honorary member of the class of 1962 even though she never graduated. I guess that maybe they needed to fill seats because so many had passed away from her class since high school.

That evening I decided to tell my mother about my abuse. I really had to psyche myself up. I had no idea why I was so stressed. "It's my own mother, for crying out loud. She's got to believe me!" I said to myself. Mother was in the next room listening to our stereo. I was in the kitchen getting dinner ready and rehearsing in my mind what I'd truly, truly like to say if I had the guts to. I'd tell her:

"Mommy, I want to show you something."

And I'd take out this frail little

four year old heart and tell her,

"I've been carrying it around in my vest

pocket for nearly twenty years."

Then I would show it to her.

It has a few bruises on it with a little lint.

You could also tell where my inexperienced hands

had tried to stitch it back together so many years ago.

"See, Mommy, remember that man down the

street he hurt me Mommy. He made me kiss

and suck on his big nasty, scary Tallywacker.

I was afraid, I choked, and I had nightmares.

Mommy, I promised him I wouldn't tell. I'm sorry

I didn't tell you so you could have rescued me, here."

I'd say as I handed her that little heart,

"I trust you. Now, please make it all better.

You can do it. You can do anything. I love you, Mommy."

Oh, how I wished I could say those words to her.

Then I'd continue. "And, see, I have another broken

heart right here in my other pocket. Here it is.

When I was eleven years old, Uncle Everett did these

things to all of us kids. He made me feel uncomfortable

and dirty. But, then I started to like it and I felt bad

about that too. You're not mad at me are you, Mother?

I didn't mean to like it!" And, if I got the chance to tell

her that, and then maybe I'd take it all the way and tell her,

"And Mom, I have another little heart too...I've been embarrassed for all these years about it.

It's kind of flat and smelly because I've hid it in my shoe. You see, it shattered into many pieces when I was on that Greyhound Bus heading to Washington when you sent me to live with my father and my wicked step-mother."

Then I'd finally tell her, "I tried to glue it back together with my tears, see." And as I'd show her, I'd work up all the courage and tell her the truth about what really happened back in the fifth grade. I just wanted to let you know that Gamin made me suck on his penis.

I so desperately needed a friend back then.

Mom, can you ever forgive me?

Mother, you're my hero!"

Alison brought me back to reality as she ran over to the stove where I had almost let dinner burn.

"Honey, are you okay?" She asked, as she took the spatula from me.

"Yeah, just a little nervous." I said.

"Well, say a little prayer before you tell her."

"Okay." I said. I told Alison that I'd tell mother after dinner during dessert while she was cleaning up the kitchen.

As soon as dinner was on the table, I put on my 'Happy Time' mask. I had to swallow my real grown up heart a couple of times, it kept getting stuck in my throat. We finished our meal and Mother and I started eating our dessert. Finally, I took a deep breath, and said a quick silent prayer and then started to speak.

"Um, Mom? I have something to share with you. Something you might not have been aware of." (Remember, mothers *always* seemed to know our every move!) "Well, it's like this..." As she sat there emotionless, I told her about Mr. Gomez and then I took her through my quick rendition of Uncle Everett's activities. By that time, I wasn't getting *any* kind of reaction from across the table. Mother just sat there eating her pudding. I was debating whether to start telling her my version of what happened with Gamin and I back in grade school, when all of a sudden, mother got up from her chair and says,

"Yes, well, I think I'll go help your wife with the dishes." She said and called out, "Alison, how's it going?"

So there I was left sitting all alone...utterly embarrassed wishing I was invisible and wanting to die.

That evening we went to the movies, not that I remembered any of it because I was in a fog. Later that night, as Alison and I got ready for bed, she asked me,

"So how did it go, telling your mother?"

"She had drop kicked my heart again." I told her. She seemed to understand what I meant. As I drifted off to sleep, I thought to myself, "Well, I'll just add this to my broken heart collection."

I couldn't even tell you anything that happened during the rest of mother's visit. I put on my 'Everything's Fine' Mask and coasted on autopilot.

That experience left me feeling totally exposed and completely empty inside. It reaffirmed the toxic view of myself. That never-ending, self-condemning voice inside me echoed, "Jim, you're a piece of crap. What happened to you was not a big deal. It was not important. Why dwell in the past, keep moving forward. Buck up and get over it already! Be a man and deal with it. Stop having a pity party all the time. It's not always about you!"

I realized from that day on, with certain people you have to keep the conversation nice and airy. "But, why does it have to be that way with my own family?" I thought to myself, "Man, I hate those

Brady Bunch people!" In time, I even learned to do that with my closer friends. I would only go as deep into a conversation as *they* took it. I never dared go so deep into my own life; because I was afraid, they would run and hide. I thought, "I feel your pain, I wish you could feel mine, too."

~

While I was writing this chapter, it dawned on me just how upset I was back then. I felt abandoned by my mother on that day, but it wasn't the first time I had that feeling of abandonment from her. When she sent me to live with my father. I hadn't realized just how far reaching it had an effect on my life. I recall when ever I'd take Alison to the bus station (it was the same one mother took me to), so Alison could go visit her family. I would be filled with anxiety and terribly upset. Reflecting back now I realize I feared that maybe I wouldn't see my wife again because I wouldn't be able to be there to protect her from harm, or maybe she'd leave me for good because I was a bad person. Even today, I hate being separated from my wife it saddens me greatly.

-CHAPTER THIRTY SEVEN-

On the Move and Hiding My Trail

*A*lison and I decided we needed a fresh start in our marriage. Things were finally smoothing out between my wife and I, we both decided it would do us good if we put a little distance between her mother and us. Rosemary and I were still having battles over control issues. Simply put, my thinking was, "She signed over those rights when I married her daughter. Alison was *my* property now." I transferred my employment to a sister company located north of Sacramento California.

My father was not pleased with our move and I never knew why. It confused me, with so many years of indifference and then to get mad at our decision to move away. "Sorry Pops, you had your chance... See ya!" Of course, I'd *never* say that to his face. Instead, I told him,

"Well, Dad. I have a job opportunity. You know a better position and more money. You understand." But truth be told, I wanted to run away from my problems. To hide my secrets and to get away from anyone who really knew me and those who would not let go of the past, or could hamper my spiritual progress. Moreover, I still longed to have a close relationship with a family member, my new job put us only a few minutes' drive away from my mother.

After we packed up all of our belongings, including a large suitcase full of all my 'masks', Alison and I headed south, from Washington state to California. One year later, I quit my job and we started our own cleaning business. At the time, I was twenty-four years old, being my own boss and working my own hours. I continued to paint houses, too.

Unfortunately, after we started this business, all the credit card company's began courting us.

"Oh look at all the money we got!" we said with glee. I soon learned that there is no such thing as *free* money.

-CHAPTER THIRTY EIGHT-

No Sitting on the Fence

𝒪ur marriage was not the only one on the rocks. My mother went back to school and got her high school diploma. Then she took some computer courses and started working outside the home. Rodger, my step-dad, felt threatened because he was from the old school where husbands work and support the family and the wives stayed home. The more mother continued to better herself, the more Rodger drank. The more she spread her wings, the more cocky and independent she became and he eventually lost his grip on her. While his wife was moving forward with the times, he was drinking more and more. He used to say to me,

"I don't drink any more than I did when I was your age." Which was a lie, but even if it were true, his fifty-four year old body wasn't able to absorb the alcohol like my twenty-five year old frame could. But, the bottom line was, he was a slave to the bottle and it was nobody's fault but his own.

One night, while he and my mother were fighting. It had been brewing for weeks. Rodger, 'The Pacifist', had had just about enough of mother. I knew she manipulated him something terrible. On that particular night, she pushed him too far, and he just snapped. He cold cocked her right in the jaw, left a bruise and everything. "Excellent."

I'm sure she thought to herself, "Now I can get rid of the drunken S.O.B. and he's gonna pay big time!" Mother called us the next day and told us that our stepfather was in jail.

"He was drunk," She said, "and he hit me and I wasn't doing nothing either." "Yeah. Okay, right!" I thought.

She manipulated us kids to choose sides. We were sucked right into the web she had so carefully woven. Unfortunately, I was at her house when Roger called from jail. He was so grateful that I was there and answered the phone. He explained what had happened and that he was truly sorry. He had just gotten tired of mother's crap. He'd also been out of sorts lately because his best friend had just died. Mother had been riding him so hard about everything. He paused for a long time before he asked,

"Can you spot me the money to bail me out, son? I've been sleeping on a picnic table down here, and it's noisy and just horrible, James." He said, "I'm really very sorry for what I did to your mother." Then, I will never forget the next moment. It felt like I was being utterly torn in two. To this day, I still feel so bad because I now realize the hell he was in, my mother was on the other phone listening in, and she looked at me with those sad helpless eyes. I paused for a long time, our eyes squarely fixed on each other like two people at the O.K. Corral. It was decision time for me. Before that moment, I had only been a spectator. But now I somehow found myself just seconds away from what I did not want to do. That little voice inside me said, "It's all or nothing Jimbo. You can't sit on the fence anymore." With our eyes still connected and a quick shake of her head, Rodger's fate was sealed.

"Dad..." I said, "I can't do that now. I, I don't have the money to spare. I'm sorry, I'm sorry. Dad, I have to go now. I'm sorry."
Rodger had never been in trouble before in his life. He was tired and scared and I just left him there. I hung my head and as I left their

house, I'll never forget her evil laugh as she said,

"Hee, hee, hee... I told you I'd get that sorry, drunken, son of a bitch!" Unfortunately, my role in this fiasco didn't end there. Mother talked me into serving Rodger their divorce papers. As I handed them to him, I looked into his eyes and I could see that his whole world collapsing all around him. He was absolutely devastated. Twenty-three years of marriage washed down the drain, just like that. I saw a single tear trickle down his face before I quickly turned and walked away.

I felt like my mother's puppet and boy did she know how to pull the strings. She was on top of the world. I, however, wanted to find a rock and crawl under it.

-CHAPTER THIRTY NINE-

"What Was I Thinking?"

While we were dealing with my parent's divorce, Alison and I were also making frequent trips up to Washington to take care of her ailing father who had Tuberculosis. Both crises were taking a toll on our marriage and our finances. There were months when we lived solely on our credit cards.

On one visit, we stayed with Rosemary and Alison's little brother, Andy, who was fourteen at the time. Our relationship was cordial. I attempted to be the male role model that he so desperately needed. He didn't have much of a chance with his mother being the president of the 'Man-Haters Club' for the State of Washington, and a shoe-in for being their C.E.O. of North America.

Andy had asthma and I had read in a health magazine, that a good massage was very beneficial to calm asthma sufferers and help their breathing. I had several friends back in Sacramento who took schooling for massage therapy, and of course, they practiced and taught me many massage techniques. So one day when Andy had experienced a rough time with his asthma, I persuaded him to let me give him a full-body massage.

I had him lay down on his stomach with nothing on but his under shorts. As I began to massage him, he started to relax and breathe easier. I, too, was calming down from my stresses and anxieties. As I moved my hands gently over his body, I started to think, "You know I really love this kid. I wish he wasn't going through such a rough time in his life. I remember when I was his age. Man, it was tough!" I continued to reason, "He has asthma. I had epilepsy. He doesn't have a father around. Mine wasn't there for me either... he's such a great kid." I certainly did not start out thinking I was going to violate his personal boundaries. I had him turn over and lay on his back. As I continued to massage him, I noticed he was getting an erection. I was shocked to see that I was having that effect on him. Regrettably, it was at that point that I started to have a desire to touch his penis. As I saw him getting aroused, I became aroused. I kept asking him if it felt good and he said,

"Yes."

Then the battle within me started. I began to rationalize, "I love him. We're family. This is not hurting him... It happened to me around his age and 'it wasn't a big deal'. This is so wrong. No, no, I can touch him and make it look like an 'accident'. Yeah, that's it." As he lay there with his eyes closed, I lightly brushed my hand over his penis. Andy took a deep breath of surprise. However, his eyes remained closed. After I did that, I instantly thought, "What the heck am I doing? Are you crazy! Have you totally lost your mind? Man that had to be the most stupid thing you've ever pulled. Now, get the heck out of his room and forget this ever happened." So I finished up and got ready to leave his room. He said thanks and that it did help his breathing. He told me he was sleepy and stayed there in his bed. After that, I felt so rotten about myself, and I prayed that Andy wouldn't think I did it on purpose. I felt like scum. My conscience and self-worth took another nose dive into my own self-made hell within.

I have since, learned that a bad conscience creates secondary victims, too. My relationship with Alison was still volatile. Doesn't every husband and wife communicate at twenty thousand decibels? One of our many recurring arguments was about having children. Alison thought that a baby would make her life complete. She longed to be needed and to be loved unconditionally, so she would have someone who relied on her. I however, wanted to prove to her, and myself, that I could be a decent husband before venturing into fatherhood. Both views were truly heartfelt and real. Looking back now, I can see we did not have the right tools or know how to give each other what the other one needed unselfishly. We never felt qualified nor worthy of respect for ourselves let alone for one another. We had been married for four years (and they said it wouldn't last). During that time, we had become dysfunctional soul mates. On our good days, we'd share our hopes, dreams, fears, and extremely intimate details from our past... Then, on our bad days, we would take that information and use it to hurt one another. She'd tell me,

"You're so stupid; at least I didn't do..." Then I'd snap back something worse.

"Oh yeah? Well, at least I hadn't..." Then it was back in her corner. She said,

"Oh? Well, at least I didn't screw the family cow!" "Ouch," I said to myself. "That's gonna leave a mark." To that I countered,

"Well, at least I didn't sleep with the whole state of Washington, you stupid whore!" I felt justified in throwing that back in her face, "She did it to me first, right?" I thought, "So there, that oughta shut her up." It did. We went back to our separate corners to lick our wounds. Did I mention that make-up sex was great? Sad though, it seemed like it was the only kind of sex we ever had. There were many times when I didn't even get that. I got so tired of begging for sex I thought, "Why does a married man have to beg his wife to have sex. Is that normal?" I was so completely fed up with my humiliating desperation. I settled for masturbating while I watched her sleep. I loved that. I got such a rush out of being sneaky. It made me feel clever and powerful. Sometimes, I fantasized about having rough and wild sex with Alison. It helped to release some of my aggressions and made me feel manly. But, then after I was done, I'd open my eyes and realize how pathetic I was. There I was, having to sneak around with 'Mr. Happy' in my hand. In reality, it made me feel weak, powerless, unmanly, and stupid. It infuriated me to realize how sad my life really was. I said to myself, "Stupid red-headed witch. No matter how hard I try to control her, she still has me by the balls. Man, I hate that!" I continued to resent her and feel vindictive.

About a year had passed since I "accidentally" touched Andy during his massage. Alison and I were still making the commute to take care of her father. While we were there, we spent a lot of time with Rosemary and Andy. Rosemary was having a hard time with Andy; he was going through a rebellious stage. She looked to me for help when I was around. There were a couple of times; I attempted to put the fear of God into him. Once he forged his mother's signature to buy video games. I happened to be there when Rosemary was going through her mail and found an unaccounted for charge of over four hundred dollars and Andy's name was on the signature for the charge. Needless to say, she hit the roof. Andy had the audacity to attempt to justify his actions and blame his mother because she had refused to buy him the video games in the first place. I couldn't believe he had done something illegal. I stepped in and took matters into my own hands. "How dare he be so disrespectful to his mother. He's insane! I've got to wise him up before he does this again, or even something worse!" I reasoned to myself.

Andy stood four inches taller than my 6' 1" frame and

weighed about 50 pounds more than I did. He started getting ignorant with me. So with an angry burst of adrenaline, I grabbed hold of him and threw him into the kitchen. Where did I learn that move? At least he didn't need stitches like I did back when my mother threw me into the cabinet door. I got his attention, all right, plus I encouraged his mother to take action and get some counseling for him. He needed to take responsibility for his crime and hopefully nip his delinquency in the bud before it spread outside the home.

Alison and I left for home a few days after I rattled Andy's cage, and, I ceased being his 'favorite' brother-in-law. I'm sure he was glad that I was his *only* brother-in-law and probably wished I wasn't even that by the time his mother got through with him. His mother grounded him and he had to figure out how he was going to pay the credit card bill at age fifteen with no job other than mowing his grandmother's lawn.

About two months had gone by and Andy was still licking his wounds over what happened. During one of his meetings with a counselor, he mentioned my "massage." That revelation concerned the counselor very much and he soon got hold of me by phone. Regrettably, I lied and I told him it was an outrage and that Andy was only trying to get back at me by ruining my good name. I said,

"Yes, I did give Andy a massage. But, even if I did brush over his penis, it was purely by accident." I was grateful that he believed me.

Ultimately, I was really glad that the issue was out in the open and that I was finally able to put it behind me. Sadly, looking back, at the time I felt clever about how I was able to get off the hook so easily. There really wasn't much love lost between Andy and I. It gave me a real reason to dislike the little snitch.

Poor Alison had to battle with her loyalty. Would she believe her husband or her baby brother? She ended up taking my word for it. I can say that in the back of her mind, she probably wouldn't have put it past me but I was so smooth and manipulative, she wouldn't dare follow her intuition. Today I'd encourage anybody to trust their gut. It is better to be too cautious then live with regret.

"What was I thinking?" was the $10,000 question that had gone unanswered all my life. I have learned that our experiences in life can propitiate our dysfunctional behavior, by first starting at our thinking and feeling process. If I stop and reflect on where such destructive thoughts come from, then I can get the answer to "What was I thinking?" Case in point, it's only within the last few years, since I've been writing my life experiences and sharing them with others in trauma healing, that I've realized what my mother did to me was horrific abuse and not "discipline." I've discovered Mr. Gomez's "affection" and attention was not love but sexual abuse. I learned that the abuse I suffered was wrong, and that it *did* have an effect on me. I have a right to expose all of those injustices I endured; I have the right and obligation to tell others how I allowed the cycle of abuse to continue due to my destructive thinking and shame. I hope that by doing so I can help others by showing them. It's never too late to stop the vicious cycle of abuse no matter what kind it is.

-CHAPTER FORTY-

Getting Off the Dead Horse

After about fifteen trips up to Washington to take care of Alison's father, he passed away at the age of seventy-three. Her father had been a glorified transient for most of his life. He drifted across the United States living with different women and doing odd jobs. He eventually retired and lived alone and got by on his meager VA pension until he died. He had only been back in Alison's life since we'd been married. It was nice for both of them and we felt good about doing the best we could for him before he passed away.

During most of those visits, Alison and I would also make the extra two-hour trip to my father's house. During those visits, I reminded myself to keep the conversation on meaningless small talk. My parents were never much into discussing anything too deep or with any kind of substance. At least not with us kids. I recall, while I was growing up, we never really talked *with* one another. We only knew how to talk *at* each other. So we'd catch up on the weather and how their jobs were going or, how they fared on their latest annual deep-sea fishing trip off Kodiak Island, Alaska. After about forty-five minutes into our visit, my father usually started showing signs of restlessness. That was our queue that he was finished with our visit. Then, like clockwork, he'd get up, stretch and complain about his bad knees and kindly remind us how he couldn't sit for very long. During the drive back to town, feelings of disappointment flooded my mind. "That's the man who can sit for hours in front of the television and watch football. Or sit and play cards or chess with his friends until late into the evening. Yet, he can't seem to be able to sit for even one lousy hour with his son that he doesn't see that often?" It was so frustrating and unfair.

Although Alison and I always made an effort to visit my folks, they however, never made efforts to visit us.

My father never even called us. I was always the one checking on them to see how things were with them and to tell them that I was still on earth and alive, just in case they were wondering. I remember now what my father's words were to me just before we moved to California. He told me,

"Son, now that you've decided to move away, I want you to know that I'm not much into writing, I never have been, and I don't like to read books let alone take the time to read letters, and I hate to talk too long on the phone, so then don't you expect to run up a phone bill."

However, the real clincher was when they traveled to Hollywood twice a year to see Leslie's brother. The interstate they took and exit ramp they had to pass was just five miles away from our house. I found it hard to accept that they could not even stop and visit for a few minutes to stretch their legs, and then be on their way again. Heck, I would have even met them on the exit if they were that pressed for time.

Well, that was it for me. I was running up against a brick wall and getting hurt every time. I finally had to take my blinders off and face reality. This relationship with my father was like beating a dead horse. It's time to get off that dead horse. If I sat there and continued to beat that poor thing to get it to move, I was only making myself look stupid.

If you find yourself in a one sided relationship, I hope that you will stop and realize just how useless your efforts are and that you are wasting time, and energy, on a relationship that is ultimately killing you. You will see that it would be more beneficial for both parties if you got up off that dead horse, dusted yourself off, and use your energy more wisely by looking for a healthier relationship, or horse to ride down life's road together into the sunset.

I finally got off that dead horse back in 1991.

-CHAPTER FORTY ONE-

Mother's Death

Since my mother's divorce, she seemed more confident and happy. She was doing the dating thing. Losing weight and attending a few single's dances. Eventually she moved in with a man who lived on fifty acres about an hour's drive east of downtown Sacramento. She became a real country girl involved in all sorts of outdoor activities. I was proud of her, as I saw a different side of her I'd never seen before. Upon looking closer, I also saw that she was scared, and sometimes, if I looked just right, I caught a glimpse of vulnerability. It made me feel good to see that my mother was human. A fact I forgot sometimes.

Through the years her motto for life had been. "I know I'm going to hell, so I live life accordingly." And, she did just that. The one thing that puzzled me about her life was, "Why do women go from one alcoholic to another?" I couldn't figure that out because my mother never smoked or drank. She lived with him for almost a year, before she ended the relationship. Then mother moved in with her oldest friend she met some twenty-five years earlier at Beauty School. As time passed, Mother slowly started to sever all of her relationships. One day, her friend came home from work and found mother huddled in a ball in a corner with a gun in her hand. She was thinking of killing herself. Fortunately, it wasn't loaded.

Mother committed herself to a mental hospital for a couple of months. Then, after she was released, she moved in with Alison and I. That put quite a strain on our already stressed marriage. It took us a while to realize what Mother was doing to our marriage; she manipulated us against each other. She was so good at that. It's what she did best. It's what mother had done to my brother Jason and I all of our lives. She pretended to be on your side, all helpful and loving, only to stab you in the back when you weren't around. She was a pro at keeping crap stirred up between her kids. Amazingly, I actually had enough sense to take Alison out of the house from time to time. We took short weekend trips, which gave us a chance to regroup and get focused again.

"Mother is not well!" I reminded my wife, "She's going through hell, and I guess she doesn't want to go there alone."

While my mother was living with us, there were occasions where I worked up the courage to ask her about the times when she "disciplined" me. I asked her what I did that was so wrong to deserve those beatings or why she got so out of control at times. Now, at the time of my questioning her, I was still convinced that it was still mainly my fault. So I was half-expecting her confirmation, "I was indeed a piece of crap and deserved every bit of what I got." But, thankfully, she never said that to my face. Her reply was always that she was sorry and that she was going through some tough times back then with Rodger and she took it out on us kids...Well, after each response, I tried to feel better, I never did.

Then, tragically, one January afternoon, we received a call from the hospital. Mother had been out driving and got disoriented; thankfully, she was able to stop on the side of the road. A Good Samaritan stopped to assist her then he called for an ambulance from his cell phone. Once she got to the hospital, they did a cat scan and found a very large brain tumor. The tumor was malignant. They immediately scheduled her for surgery. Unfortunately, the doctors were not able to remove the entire tumor. Right after surgery, the doctor said everything went fine and she came through pretty well, considering her condition. They hoped chemo and radiation treatments would slow down the cancer's progress. Nevertheless, they gave her about six months to a year to live. The doctors at the mental hospital took a cat scan of mother just five months earlier. Unfortunately, the scan was from her nose down. Why didn't they do her whole dang blasted head for crying out loud? They might have caught the cancer in time, and it would have answered a lot of questions as to why mother was acting the way she was and why she suffered with terrible migraines. I was infuriated at the negligence of her former doctors. Words truly cannot describe how completely livid I was. Then, almost five days after her surgery, she was alert and looking around. I went out and bought her a new walkman and an Ann Murray tape. She was mother's favorite singer. She listened to the songs, while I fed her ice chips. Later that evening, her condition took a turn for the worse. The doctors said she was doing fine, but that she simply shut herself down. My mother died three days later, nine days after she entered the hospital. Even though I watched her take her last breath, I truly think my mother died alone.

In all my twenty-seven years, that was the saddest day of my life. "Anybody else passing away is better than losing your mother. Mothers are the family rock. They keep the families together. Her opinion was gold. She was God! But then I realized, 'and yet she just gave up, just like that…" I was so incredibly sad and angry with her at the same time. Then I felt guilty because I knew that I was being selfish. I knew that my baby brother Jerry, who was only seventeen, was hurting worse than I was. Then I finally remembered that she had been in tremendous pain for some time and at least now she was not suffering and was safe in God's memory and I would see her again.

My step-dad and I made amends and worked together on mother's eulogy. I was privileged to deliver it at her memorial service held at a friend's home. About forty of our closest friends attended. After the service, we played some of her favorite music. To this day, I still cannot listen to any of Ann Murray's songs. My mother was only forty-nine years old when she fell asleep in death.

After her death, I went through all of her personal belongings. I stumbled across some papers she had from her stay at the mental hospital. Part of her treatment there included various writing exercises. For example, she was asked to describe her view of each of her family members. I read it and when I got down to my name, I read, "James is a real thorn in my side." "Ouch…" I cannot even begin to explain how completely devastated and hurt I felt. I paused for a long time and then thought, "Can somebody please help me? My heart is breaking here!" How ironic—my mother was able to dropkick my heart even from the grave… man she was good!

Eventually, I was able to move on and acknowledge that I really did do well in my taking care of her for the last few months of her life. I viewed it as a blessing. But, then I put my sarcasm mask on. "A real blessing, uh?" I asked myself, "The faithful nurse maid to the end. Jimbo the martyr." I scoffed, and then I asked myself, "So really, what choice did she have but to give up? Maybe she would have gotten a little better, but for what, to live her last remaining months with the 'Son from Hell', the thorn in her side, 'Mr. Thorn Man'?" I had to reason, "My mother truly was not a happy camper, so why should anyone else be?"

-CHAPTER FORTY TWO-

On the Move (Again)

Within twelve months time, Alison lost her father and I had lost my mother. One bright spot during this dark period was when we befriended Bernie and Dorothy Garrison. We decided to move to Kansas with Garrisons. They were a lovely couple. Dotty was like the mother I never had. She loved Alison and I very much and we became inseparable. Dotty was able to show love without the head games and manipulations. She didn't expect anything in return. She was loving, kind, and loyal. I felt safe being around her, I could be myself and Alison could be herself too, and I wasn't embarrassed by it. Dotty was the one who taught me that it was okay for Alison to be Alison and that it wasn't a bad reflection on me, and if she wanted people to see that her elevator was a little slow, well then that was on her and not me. I was so relieved because I had finally found the family I'd been looking for all my life.

They were moving to Kansas because of Bernie's work. Alison and I planned the move thoroughly. We worked hard and saved some money. We bought a twenty-four foot travel trailer, we sold everything we had and lived in it for a few months before heading to the Midwest. We had enough money to live off for about three months until we were settled. We also had our credit cards. Since we made sure to make the minimum payments on time, our credit was pretty good and they extended the amount we could charge. I thought, "Hey, this is great! Look at all the money we have. We can live off these things for six months if we had to. Life will be grand!" The cards made me feel like I was in control of my destiny. "I can do anything and go anywhere," I reflected. "Why just last year Alison and I took a much needed vacation. We cruised to Jamaica and it didn't cost us any money out of our pockets. In fact, we saved hundreds because we used our plastic."

At that time, Alison and I were even having less make-up sex and more 'just because I love you' sex. Shoot, I was feeling so good; Alison talked me into getting a dog. I chose to purchase, a purebred Shar Pei.

"Do you take plastic? No? That's okay; I'll just go get a cash advance." Mr. Plastic was our friend, at twenty-two percent interest rates.

Alison and I settled into our new town and we were quickly making new friends. Our dear friends, Bernie and Dotty, moved into a luxury condominium just a few minutes away from Topeka, where he worked as a postmaster.

Alison and I moved to Kansas in 1993. We found a little community to live in. It was about a half hour drive south of Kansas City, called Stanley. We found it hard to find jobs that paid enough to keep up with our bills. We had six credit cards and most were maxed out during our trip across the country. We started to receive late notices. The collective interest alone was seven hundred dollars a month.

Alison and I started fighting again it was what we knew. We soon learned that when you make a move, the only thing that changes is your location not your problems. Our dysfunction followed us. Sadly, it felt comfortable to be back to 'normal' in our dysfunctional relationship.

We eventually landed some jobs to make ends meet. I cooked at an old Stuckey's Restaurant on the weekends. In addition, we both were hired as school bus drivers. That worked out perfect for us, because we needed to update our driver's licenses anyways. Driving a bus route for a couple of hours a day worked out great.

I was a little nervous about driving a huge vehicle, but my biggest fear was how to deal with watching that many kids all at the same time. Alison and I had friends with children, but when we were around them, they had to be on their best behavior. Sometimes we even took kids for the weekend. We took them to the movies, or to the Mall. We spoiled them, and filled them up with sugar, then returned them to their rightful owners. But, this was going to be completely different.

I remembered my own bus riding days. Most of the kids weren't exactly what you would call saints. But I felt up for the challenge, and I thought, "Well, at least I won't have to pay for my licenses and training. This should be quite a learning experience." I told myself, "It's only a few hours a day. Besides, I have a CB just in case I run into a problem."

I drove a bus route for two years. I was actually sad when I had to quit but I really needed a full time job to pay bills. However, overall, the kids were great. I had developed a nice rapport with them, just like I remembered I had with my own bus driver when I was in school.

Driving that school bus proved to be quite a learning experience as well as a wonderful blessing. I learned how to stay in control of sixty plus students in grades K thru twelve all at the same time. My self-esteem skyrocketed, "Would you look at me! I can drive this yellow beast and take care of all these children without pulling my hair out or wanting to kill them." I learned the **'broken record technique' and found that I was able to stay calm and still get what I needed to get the job done. Recently I ran across that technique in the book 'Adult Children of Abusive Parents' by Steven Farmer, on page 87 under subtitle, 'broken record.' Before that experience, I had never felt worthy enough to have children of my own. I was in fear of hurting them like my parents had hurt me. But, after that experience, I thought maybe I *could* be a good father after all. But I stopped and remembered who their mother would be. Then I realized that I still needed to be a better husband.

** 'Broken Record technique definition is found in the last subtitle of the chapter 'Rules in Fighting Fair'.

-CHAPTER FORTY THREE-

"I'm Fine, Take Me Home!"

One cold and snowy night in January, after my shift at the restaurant, I hitched a ride with Janice, a fellow employee. The roads were extremely slick and Janice lost control of her car. We fishtailed and spun like a top before another car hit us on my side of the vehicle. I ended up with a several broken ribs and a collapsed lung. I spent five days in the hospital. I absolutely hated it there because it reminded me of when my mother died. The oxygen they use at the hospital permeated the air. The smell made me nauseated and very depressed. I had trouble breathing. It felt as if I was taking in breaths of death. "This is what death smells like." I said to myself, "I don't want to die!" Then I begged my wife,

"Please take me home. I'm doing fine. Take me out of here, please!" Every day when the doctors asked,

"How are we doing today, Mr. Petra?" I'd tell them with a big smile,

"I'm doing fine!" I was all teeth as I had my 'Happy Time' mask on, polished and shining bright. But then they touched me, the pain sent me through the roof. I was so emotional that when friends came in to see me, I started crying and begging them to take me home, and Alison wasn't listening to me. I just wanted to get far, far away from that smell of death.

When friends weren't there, Alison and I continued our arguments. We had been fighting about something even before the accident and now I was depressed and in so much pain. She was getting fed up with my Jekyll and Hyde personality and was irritated with all my masks. Our criticism and sarcasm was getting more and more malicious. She had grown tired of being my personal whipping post. One day she confided in one of our older friends, saying that as soon as I was well enough and back on my feet that she was going to leave me.

Well, if things were not already bad enough, during my stay at the hospital our pipes froze and broke in our travel trailer. So when I was released from the hospital, our good friends, the Mendoza's, offered to let us stay with them until our trailer was in order. We stayed with them for a couple of months. I was so grateful to have such wonderful friends. While we lived with our friends, Alison and I still found ways to bicker. Only we used whispers and deadly stares. I thought, "Just you wait until we're back at home. You are so in trouble!"

Eventually the weather warmed up we got our trailer fixed and moved back in. I was laid up and out of work for six months and in excruciating pain and extremely grouchy. I guess, just like mother, I didn't want to be miserable alone.

I was so stressed because our bills were mounting. Collection agencies were calling us daily and sending death threats. My former jobs were physical labor. I started freaking out, "What if I can't support my family, my God, what am I going to do? I'm not smart enough to find a job where I have to use my head for a living." I was scared to death and stressing, "Oh man, Alie is not bright enough to get any kind of good paying job. She doesn't even have a G.E.D. how on earth am I going to pull this off?"

Financially we somehow made it through this crisis. The collection agencies were happy to get just whatever we were able to send their way until I got back on my feet again. I slowly went back to driving my bus route and cooking at the truck stop, plus doing odd jobs like cleaning and painting. When we received the settlement money from the insurance company, we put it to good use. We finished paying the hospital bills and we bought a house. Alison and I had lived in that twenty-four foot trailer for a year and a half, along with our cat and dog. We refinanced our house and paid off twenty-four thousand dollars worth of credit card bills. We still had a little money left over to furnish our new house.

We were out of the woods financially, and our relationship improved a little, but not much. There was too much water under the bridge. Too many hurtful words exchanged, and too many emotional scares that refused to heal. Our marriage had truly become a war zone with no winners. We were both the losers.

-CHAPTER FORTY FOUR-

Crushing Alison's Spirit

One particular fight I had with Alison is forever etched in my mind. I cringe as I think about how I treated her. I don't recall what topic we were fighting about, but I do remember being violently enraged and I knew better than to lay a hand on her. So I looked for something that belonged to her to destroy. "Ah, her precious plant." I smiled with glee as I picked up. Alison's beautiful rubber tree plant that stood three foot tall. She had that plant for two years. It came with us from California. I took it into where she was and proceeded to talk to her in that low methodical voice. The same tone I had used when I threatened to kill her dog. It seemed like a lifetime ago, but it worked again, I got her attention. I thought. "Good, you redheaded, green-eyed witch, I may not be able to touch you, but I still own you and you will obey me!" I was vehemently filled with disgust and seething with complete hatred towards her. She had that beautiful plant for two years. It came with us from California.

With each word I spoke, I broke off a leaf from her prized possession and said, "Now, you listen to me and you listen good. You (I clipped a leaf off) will (clipped another) mind (clip) me and do (clip) as (clip) I (clip) say!" I clipped and clipped and clipped until no beautiful leaves remained on that poor plant. I watched and saw her spirit break with every snap of a leaf. She turned back into putty right before my eyes. I felt in control again, like a god.

"I'm still the man of this house," I told her, "and I will prevail!" With that, I turned and walked away and dropped the plant next to her sobbing, crumpled body in the hallway.

To be sure, there was no make-up sex that night, even after I apologized profusely for my earlier cruelty. "Maybe I did go a little overboard." I thought to myself, "I had better give her a little space for awhile." Then I got mad at myself. "Yes sir. You're a real man destroying that plant. Man, I hate myself." However, then I tried to justify my actions, "I wish Alison would just listen to me!" But try as I may, I still felt like scum, like real worm food.

Soon enough, we were back on speaking terms. She and I were civil but the mood was somewhat solemn for a couple of weeks after the plant episode. Personally, I didn't mind the atmosphere in the house. At least we weren't screaming down each other's throat. I still felt bad, but slightly justified. "Hey, it's good to be the king." I said to myself. "She just needed another reminder, that's all."

So throughout those weeks, we still were not having sex. I was tolerant at first, but as the days dragged on, I found myself doing what I'd done all our married life, begging and begging, then more begging… I started to get miffed, again, as I began to think, "Enough already, it's time to move on!" I wanted to say, "Come on, let's snap out of it! The past is the past, so buck up, and stop having a pity party." But I didn't dare tell her. However, I started to reason, "It wasn't that bad. I didn't physically hurt her. It was just a stupid plant." I was so callused and devoid of compassion.

One particular night, as we were getting ready to retire for the evening, I asked my despondent wife,

"Are the moons aligned tonight so I can 'have some' this evening

Alie sugar, sweetheart?"

"No, no, not even close." She said.

"Well," I tried again, "is it our anniversary?" I asked because she was most willing during the month of our anniversary.

"No, but nice try." She replied, "Why don't you just go jack yourself off in the bathroom because 'it' ain't happening tonight." Oh, man, I got so furious. We knew all too well how to push each other's buttons. I thought, "How dare she talk to me like that." I was so humiliated and embarrassed. "Okay," I said to myself, "Stay cool and keep your 'Everything's Under Control' mask on." I was still in great need for intimacy. It had been well over two weeks since the plant episode. "It's my right as a husband." I reasoned with myself. "She's denying me sex and it's not right!" So I pestered and begged her for three hours straight. "How dare she suggest I go masturbate!" I told myself, "I've waited long enough. I'm a man; I have needs to be met." So I continued to beg,

"Pleeease!"

"Oh, alright already, geez." She finally said, "I'm tired of hearing you beg. I need to get some sleep. Here—." Then she laid there like a slab of frozen meat.

"Hurry up, are you done yet? Are you done yet?" she kept asking. I was so worked up in need of sex, but now that she let me, especially since she was acting like that, just laying there stiff as a board and not even faking she loved me I was humiliated.

"Hurry up. Are you done yet?" She continued without let up. I don't know how I concentrated enough to finish, but I did. After that, I went over to my wallet, found a few dollars, and threw it on the bed.

"Here," I said to her in disgust, "for services rendered. This is how you made me feel and that's all you're worth you stupid whore!" I went to the bathroom. I could hear her crying softly. "Oh, sure," I said to myself, "Now she shows emotions!" I started to hate myself for having no self-control. "Man, if Alie were to cut my penis off like Lorena Bobbitt, I wouldn't even blame her. I hate being a slave to it. I hate begging for sex. I hate masturbating. God, I hate myself. I hate myself..." As I went to the kitchen to get a drink of water, I heard Alison in the bathroom. We met in the bedroom where neither one spoke or had eye contact. We were both hurt deeply and humiliated beyond repair. We laid as far away from each other as humanly possible, we finally both drifted off into miserable sleep.

That was the last time I had sex with my wife. Two weeks later, while I was at work, she packed up all that she could carry and caught a greyhound bus heading to Washington. When I got home, I found a short note from her saying that she couldn't take it anymore. I wasn't too surprised though. Even I couldn't stand myself.

I assumed Alison just needed a break for a few weeks. She hadn't seen her mother since we moved to Kansas. I figured she went to visit and regroup. "Super." I said to myself, "I needed a break, too." It was nice to have the house to myself, it was quiet, and stress free for a while-------but my wife didn't come back.

~

I have learned two things in recovery, one I've mentioned in the footnote section under chapter three and that is.

"Compliance is not the same as consent."

The other thing I've learned is this:

"No *always* means no. It has never meant yes or even maybe."

These two things are boundary issues, by learning to respect these issues I have learned to respect myself.

In addition, you rarely recover from calling a loved one a stupid whore. I did twice and we paid the price. So *IF* you are blessed with another relationship, clean up your thoughts of women, clean up your mouth. No one deserves to be called a demoralizing name of any kind.

~By *dignifying others, you dignify yourself.*

-CHAPTER FORTY FIVE-

Suicide Attempt Number Two

Alison had been gone for three months and I was not doing well. I hated being alone, even *I* hated my own company. I was way out of my element because the singles life was so foreign to me. So there I was, she ultimately had total control over me and my future. I realized I never really had absolute control over her and I believe that is why we fought the way we did. I have since learned that, "The one, who loves less, controls the most." And that was me for over nine years. Now she was in the driver's seat with definite plans of never looking back.

I began to slip into a deep depression. I thought, "I will never survive being single. I'm doomed!" I was lonely and embarrassed that my wife had left me. I hated to admit it, but she was my entire identity. I couldn't find my 'Everything's Under Control' mask, or my 'Happy Time' mask. Alison must have packed them and taken them with her. I was so heartbroken, I thought, "Yeah our marriage was hell, but at least it was *my* hell!" I started to hate myself even more. "I'm a failure, and a phony. I am scum of the earth." I wasn't eating right. I was also working several jobs to make ends meet. "You know," I started to reflect; "she really wasn't that bad. She really did contribute to our marriage. Man, I was such a jerk of a husband." There was no light at the end of the tunnel as far as my future. At twenty-nine years old, I was doomed to stay single for the rest of my life and I was *not* going to do that! I thought, "You know, I'd rather kill myself than be alone, and boy will she feel bad... But, if I fail and she finds out then she'll see that I can't live without her and that I love her, then she'll come back!" (Forever the manipulator, I must have inherited that talent from my mother.)

At one point, I hadn't eaten for almost a week. I continued to isolate myself. I called in sick to work. I never saw my friends. Then one typical night of insomnia, I started looking around the house to see what I could take to end my pathetic life. I found and took two hundred and fifty aspirin along with a half bottle of 'Ny Quil' for a chaser. Well by mid-morning I was still alive, I knew this because the ringing in my ears was excruciating as I bowed to the porcelain god.

Dottie had been attempting to reach me all week. She knew that I was sinking further into depression and sensed something was wrong that morning when she called and I finally answered the phone and sounded like death. She quickly called a friend who lived a few blocks away from me. He came over and took me to the hospital. They ran tests, and then fed me a disgusting charcoal drink to absorb the toxins.

They must have thought that maybe I just wanted some attention. "You can't die from taking aspirin, silly!" I heard the hospital staff talking to each other. There I was again, in a hospital breathing in that stench of death. I thought, "Isn't there anywhere they can put me without being around those oxygen tanks?" The doctor making her rounds asked,

"How are you doing Mr. Petra?"

"Fine, fine, now, thanks." I said, "I'm much better." I thought, "Get me the heck out of here, will you?" But said,

"Boy that sure was stupid of me, I sure am hungry... yes I'm fine!" I was soon released and I couldn't seem to get to the parking lot fast enough. I was having an anxiety attack. I needed fresh, clean, natural air to cleanse my lungs. I said to myself, "I thought you wanted to die? You stupid blockhead, you're such a loser!"

After my weak attempt to end my life, my friends lovingly checked in on me regularly and kept me busy. "Maybe I did need the attention." I told myself, "Hey, nobody told me I couldn't die from overdosing on aspirin. I guess I watch too much television.

2 Peter 2:22

Not long after my suicide attempt I learned that Alison was having an affair with one of her old boyfriends she had way back when she was fifteen years old. I thought, "Talk about a dog returning to its vomit!" He was still stuck in his addictions and she went right back to her true love. It made me feel like I'd been used for ten years. Then, I wondered who she was thinking of for the past nine years during our lovemaking.

When Alison called me to tell me about her affair, I felt embarrassed and humiliated. "Wait, wait!" I suddenly thought, "Did she just say I have grounds for divorce? Oh man, I am so outta here! Crud... if only I'd have waited a couple more weeks before taking those stupid aspirins, I wouldn't be stuck with this stupid hospital bill!" But, I was still feeling lost and truly longing for another chance to try to make things work out between us. I told her I'd forgive her. Then she started to cry because she couldn't believe it.

"You must truly love me, don't you?" she said.

"Of course I do. That's what I've been trying to tell you for months." I said.

"Well, maybe we can take it real slow and start courting again and see how it goes." She said with a sniffle. Something inside me just snapped,

"Oh hell no! I need you to come back *now*! We've been married for nine years. What's up with this courting stuff? We have bills to pay. I'm drowning in debt."

In her gut, she must have realized that I'd hadn't changed and never would.

"Maybe that was a bad idea." She said as I heard her hang up the phone. That was the last time I ever talked to Alison.

Sadly, I too had to agree with her. It would have been a bad idea. I truly had no clue on how to fix this marriage. For a brief moment, I felt bad for her.

Just Another Statistic

Later that week I went to a bookstore and picked up a 'Do It Yourself Divorce' book. I found out that it's a lot easier, and cheaper to get unhitched than it was to get hitched. Nothing was contested since we didn't have any children and she left without wanting anything, but her personal effects, I even got custody of our dog and cat. That book was thorough.

I stood before the judge as my own attorney. Alison didn't show up. Bernie and Dotty were in the back silently supporting me. Dottie's heart was breaking as mine was because she loved both of us. As I stood there by myself, I could not remember a more heart-wrenching day in my life.

That day surpassed the day my mother shipped me out when I was eleven. It was worse than graduation night. Or when I told my mother about Mr. Gomez and Uncle Everett. That day was even far worse than when mother passed away. Why, because all of those events really weren't my fault, I could blame somebody else for those heartbreaks. However, the day I stood alone in front of that judge was far more horrific to me because it was *my* relationship. *My* dissolution of marriage, *my* failure, and *my* fault that the last ten years were going down the drain. I was destitute and utterly embarrassed because I was moments away from being just another statistic, another number in the pile of dissolved marriages gone by the wayside.

I was days shy of being thirty years old and I was nothing special. I hadn't accomplished anything to make anybody proud of me. I felt lonely and exposed standing before the judge that day. Then after we left the courthouse, I started to play 'the blame game' "Damn women, anyways." I thought to myself, "Man I hate them. I hate them all! They make me sick!"

Not Missing a Beat

A week later, I received a refund check from the courthouse. Since I did everything myself, the divorce didn't cost me as much as they asked for up front.

The ink on the divorce papers had barely dried before I went on my first date with Tara. I was so lonely and starved for companionship, I had convinced myself, "I'm going to be a better man now. I've learned my lesson."

I met Tara through mutual friends. On our first date, I thought she was such a breath of fresh air. At dinner, she sparkled like a diamond as she strolled through the room. She could captivate the stars and hypnotize the moon. Tara was so filled with positive energy; I couldn't help but desire to tap into that. I didn't even mind picking up the tab for the whole evening. That divorce refund sure came in handy.

-CHAPTER FORTY SIX-

Poor Thinking Leads to Poor Choices

After my divorce, I sold the house and moved into an apartment. I spent all of my free time with the Mendoza family. I felt very blessed to have their support. Raphael and Angelica knew how difficult it was for me after Alison left. Raphael and Angel had eight children. I was truly a part of their family, through their good times and bad. I had observed and thought, "How unfair it is to the older boys to have so much responsibilities put on them to take care of the younger ones. That just isn't right." I was perturbed with Raphael and Angel for this but I never said anything to them.

I was extremely depressed about my current situation. "I can't stand how life had dealt me this tough hand. Stupid, phony religious beliefs, why can't people live them instead of just preach them. Marriage is supposed to last 'til death do us part' and we're supposed to be loving and respectful to each other. Nobody ever is, and I hate that. Stupid women anyways!"

I wasn't angry with God but I was mad at my mother, step-mom, Alison and her mom, and to add to that list, I was frustrated at my friend Angelica for how she treated her boys. I began to view my plight in life as one of them. I spent most of my time with the four older boys. The twins Marco and Michael were sixteen years old. Juan was fourteen, and Roberto was twelve. The more I was around them the more I thought back to *my* childhood years and *my* unfair treatment. I wanted to be there for the boys. I was the understanding one.

As I observed their unfair treatment, I couldn't help but reflect back to my own upbringing. I said to myself, "You know, if I could just return to those troubling, struggling years with what I know now, I wouldn't have kept my mouth shut when my father and step-mom preached one thing and lived another." I really resented them for that. With each passing thought, I found myself growing angrier. "Man, the guilt, and shame in the Petra house was like poisonous air that choked my very soul, I hated it. How dare them. Oh, God, I wish I could go back in time and reclaim my life. I was cheated out of a happy childhood. It's just not fair" I grieved, "It's just not fair, and life is not fair right now!" Look at how these poor boys are treated." I fumed within, "How dare their parents shame them like my folks did me." Then I came up with a solution. "Well, we'll just going to have to stick together to get through this and that's all there is to it. We'll have to look out for each other. It's us against the world." That was my true thinking. A spirit of survival and self-preservation over took me. "I must take care of number one, because you can't rely on anybody else to do it. They'll use you, and spit you right out without blinking an eye."

During this same time, I started reminiscing about what I learned during my own adolescent years. I was taught that masturbation was the answer for stress relief. Unfortunately, I took up my adolescent ways again. I fantasized about having sex with Alison on those rare times when we made love because we loved each other. But, when I remembered all the make-up sex we had during our nine years of marital hell, which infuriated me.

I made it a habit of volunteering to watch the Mendoza's kids, to give their mom a break. Raphael was usually at work most of the

182

time. Since I hated being alone in an empty room all by myself, I slept in my sleeping bag on the floor in the older boys' room. We had some fun times. I could tell by the glow on their faces that they were thrilled to have a grownup take an interest in them. I listened to their dreams and their fears. I was always there for them. I, too, thought that they were treated unfairly and I told them so. I was on their side.

I was so starved for human contact, for the human touch. As the boys were by human nature, so there were lots of hugs, play wrestling and arms around shoulders as we talked through the days and into nights. We even told stories with the lights out in their bedroom just like camping.

When I wasn't with the Mendoza family, I was spending a lot of time with Tara. We were soon discussing wedding plans. I was pouring on the charm. I wanted to get married like yesterday and she was thinking about taking a year to get to know each other and to plan the wedding. Her reasoning was,

"What will people think if we just rush into it?"

"It's not like we're teenagers. We're grown adults and we're not getting any younger." I told her. Ultimately, Tara had the final say and that infuriated me. I showed her that I was quite upset about her decision, but I did not dare lead on to just how livid I was and the outrage I felt. The changing of her mind at will meant she had total control and I just snapped. I thought, "This woman is just like *all* the rest of the female persuasion." I'd had enough of not being in control of anyone, and at that moment, it was Tara's decision, along with the attitude of mine. I was way out of my comfort zone. I was longing to be married and all of the "benefits" that went with it. I thought I needed to be married in order to have an identity and a sense of pride. When my first marriage was over, I felt like a failure. I didn't know what co-dependence was at the time, but I had a sickly form of it. In the wake of Alison's rejection and our divorce, then when Tara postponed the wedding, it was just much more than I could handle at the time. I promised myself right then. "I will *never* be hurt or ruled over like that again. I've got needs. I've got to take care of number one.

-CHAPTER FORTY SEVEN-

Looking Out for #1 at Any Cost

Of the four Mendoza kids, I spent more time with Juan. He was the middle child, like me. He wasn't old enough for the extra privileges like his older brothers were given, yet he had more chores than his younger siblings did. Juan seemed to be floundering, struggling for his own identity and acceptance, much as I did at his age. I thought, "Man, it must really be tough for Juan. I know exactly what he's going through. Life was so unfair for me too. I want to make sure he feels loved, and appreciated. I want to make sure he doesn't feel isolated or feel like he doesn't belong, like I did at his age."

Juan often talked to me in confidence. I'd put my arm around him and gently caress his back as we talked. I always asked if it felt good.

"Yes, but it tickles." I did this a handful of times and each time I'd ask him if it felt good, when he said yes that made what I was doing okay in my mind. Before long, he was desensitized to my touch, and relaxed. This was all part of the grooming process. So, by the time I molested Juan, we were already in a routine and his barriers were down.

One such opportunity was while I was helping the Mendoza's paint their house. I kept thinking of a way to get Juan alone so I could give him a massage, and really show him I cared. I thought, "Hey, I've got a huge army tent. The weather is great and I'll just ask Ralph and Angel if the kid's and I can camp out in the back yard."

The parents agreed and that night, we were all in our sleeping bags. I made sure that Juan was right next to me. We had just put in a big day of prepping the house for painting. So everyone was very tired and had no problem drifting off to sleep. I started caressing Juan's back as he lay on his stomach. I whispered,

"Does this feel good?"

"Yes." he replied. Eventually I eased down to his legs as I kept asking "How bout now?" to which he'd say,

"Yes." Therefore, I rationalized in my mind, "Then this is okay. I'm not hurting Juan. He likes it. I'm getting closer to him and showing Juan that I love him and I'll be there for him and I won't ever abandon him." These feelings made me feel powerful. I asked Juan to turn over. Then I caressed his chest, stomach and moved towards his legs while "unintentionally" touching his penis. Juan finally fell asleep, but his body was still reacting to my touching him. All the time I was thinking, "He likes it. This is okay." I felt aroused and excited.

At that point, I realized I was at a crossroads. I could stop now, he was still asleep, and on the other hand, I could pursue a course that I knew was wrong. Dead wrong! I laid there for a while reflecting back in time. I knew it was wrong when it was done to me, when I was his age, and even way younger. I had been battling with my fleshly weakness since before Juan was born. At times, I even hated my desires and prayed to God to help me control myself and to stop masturbating. I was constantly riddled with shame and guilt that stemmed from a bible thumping step-mother. However, then I rationalized my sick desires. I remembered the day I told mother about my sexual abuse. I thought, "You know what? What happened to me was no big deal. I turned out just fine. This was the only love and affection I ever got as a child and now I want to show Juan that I love him, too." I justified my actions and I crossed the line. I made the wrong choice. I fondled Juan while he slept until he ejaculated. He awoke and was suddenly anxious as he came down from the new and strange feelings of the climax. As he sat up, I asked him,

"Are you okay?" He said nothing as he got up to go outside of the tent. I nervously stammered,

"I'm sorry, I'm sorry!" I thought I was a dead man, but he said,

"Okay, I have to go pee." He came back and went straight to sleep. I on the other hand did not sleep a wink because I was so stressed.

The next morning, I was so scared that Juan would tell. Everyone eventually woke up and got ready for breakfast. I pulled Juan aside before he went into the house and I told him that I was very, very sorry. He told me that he was okay.

We continued painting the house. It took us two weekends to complete the project and nothing came out, Juan never came forward about what had happened. After that incident, you can bet I was the nicest friend anyone would have towards the whole family, but especially towards Juan. I gave him treats and hamburgers, you name it, it was his. I even called their house most everyday or I'd show up to see if all was well.

I also learned that first night in the tent, when I was fondling Juan, he told me that he and his uncle did that, too. So that information helped my abusing him further. "Oh" I thought, "Well at least I didn't start this." He was already conditioned. A slight part of me felt cheated. "I wanted to be his teacher." There were times when I even caught Juan and his uncle in the act. They were sly about it, but I knew what to look for. His uncle's actions made it easier to rationalize my relationship with Juan.

My fiancée Tara finally decided to go back to our original wedding date. We were married after just six short months of courting. My faith in the whole marriage concept, commitment, and faithfulness was still pretty slim. However, I vowed to myself that after Tara and I were married, I would never touch Juan again.

-CHAPTER FORTY EIGHT-

My Wedding Day Blues (Again)

One year to the day of Alison walking out on me, I was walking down the aisle with my new bride. It was a beautiful wedding. Tara and I were both thirty-one years old, she had been in eight wedding parties before her own, and now this was her day. I was happy and honored to be the man she'd been waiting to give herself to. I kept thinking about the whole ceremony thing. I would have settled for the courthouse drive through sermon. It would have been quicker... not to mention cheaper. Then I remembered. "This isn't my day now, is it? It's not always about me. Oh, thank God, I'm not wearing white! My goodness, Tara looks so very pretty in her white gown, so clean, pure, and elegant, just like she is. I am sooo unworthy." I felt blessed and yet ashamed of myself at the same time. I kept remembering my past and what a rotten husband I was to, 'what's her name'. That's what I had come to call Alison. I was still so resentful towards her that I couldn't stand to say her name. In addition, I thought what a hypocrite I was standing there next to this pure wholesome princess, while I knew I had committed such sinful acts with an innocent child. Nonetheless, I glued my 'Happy Time' and 'Everything is alright' mask on and rationalized. "It's okay, I only touched Juan twice. Now that I'm married, it won't happen again. The past is the past; I'll just forget it ever happened."

Tara and I were both nervous, of course, on our wedding night. She told me shyly that she wasn't too worried because she knew that I'd teach her all she needed to know. When Tara said that, I instantly flashed back to what seemed a lifetime ago. I thought of 'What's Her Names' statement on our wedding night and how it made me feel. How it *still* made me feel. Then I gently took Tara into my arms and told her,

"Princess, we'll learn together." I felt better about myself, better about life. I just knew I was going to be a better husband.

-CHAPTER FORTY NINE-

Still Looking Out for #1

*T*hat vow I made to myself about never molesting Juan again didn't last long. I selfishly reasoned, "You know, the honeymoon won't last forever, and I'll be damned if I'll beg for sex again." So I selfishly kept my options open.

I continued to spend a lot of time with Juan and his family. Every chance we got, Juan and I fondled one another through our clothes; sneaking touches here and there. When we did get together alone, we'd masturbate each other, then we slowly advanced to oral sex.

I was so sick and calculating that I made sure Juan would satisfy me first so that he'd stay interested in pleasing me. If I did him first, then he'd lose interest and or guilt would creep in and he'd leave the room. There were times however, when Juan didn't want to get together. Especially after, he turned fifteen.

The Mendoza's had been looking for new carpet for their house. I ran across some carpet that was still in good condition, so I arranged to have the boys help me retrieve it. I thought, "This will be another great opportunity to get Juan alone again." However, on the way there, I noticed that Juan was acting cold and distant. I could tell something was weighing on his mind. So as we were working away on the carpet I pulled him aside. Juan informed me that he didn't want to get together with me anymore. I felt sad, but I understood his decision. Then he said, very seriously to me,

"James, you won't kill me now will you? Since I want to quit what we've been doing?" At that moment, my heart just broke for him. I thought, "Oh, my God, the courage it must have taken to finally say 'No more!' " I calmly told him that I was fine with stopping and that he'd been watching too many movies. I gave him a reassuring hug and sent him on his way.

So that was the end of our "relationship," for the time being anyway.

Thinking "Nobody is Getting Hurt" Becomes a Lie

Tara and I had our share of arguments like most newlyweds. They say a good woman brings out the best in a man. Well she certainly had her work cut out for her. Tara calmly asked,

"Honey, why do you have to yell all the time?"

"I'm not yelling," I retorted, "I'm discussing and just talking."

"No, you're yelling and I can hear just fine, thank you."

"Oh... that's cool, okay," I said. She didn't take offense and she didn't make me feel bad about myself. Wow, this is different," I thought, "We've been married a year now, when does the honeymoon end?" I was pleased with our lives thus far but still cautious and untrusting. Tara was smart too. She noticed a pattern in my moods was connected with my diet. Through research she found out, I had low blood sugar and intolerance to M.S.G. Both of these conditions contributed to my tyrant like behavior. Tara encouraged me to eat better and take vitamins. I was banned from coffee and refined sugar and I started to feel so much better. I could concentrate better and I didn't feel so stressed and strung out all of the time. I had more energy and life was grand. I was a little more tolerable to be around but I was still a butthead at times, but just a friendlier, more cooperative one.

Truthfully, though, my life really wasn't all that grand. I was riddled with the guilt from abusing Juan. I still had tons of old baggage left over from my first marriage, and my "wonderful" childhood. I was fighting tooth and nail with a loving woman who just wanted to get close to me and love me and yet I was still suspicious of her. "Don't let her hurt you James; she's just like the rest of the control freaks, whiners, and naggers." I was selfish and deceptive. In Tara's eyes, our relationship was strained and our communication was nil. But, in my eyes, it was a cakewalk, compared to my last marriage from hell. And it wasn't like I had to beg her for sex either, because despite the turmoil, Tara loved me and enjoyed making love to me most anytime. Selfishly, that wasn't enough for me because I frequently stopped by the Mendoza's on the way home from work. And I'd always work it out so that Juan and I could sneak off somewhere and masturbate each other. All the while, I told myself, "I love this guy. He's a great, young adult. I'm teaching him how to truly show somebody he loves them." Then afterwards I went home to a wanting wife and never missed a beat. Tara and I had sex as if nothing else was going on. I even sometimes thought of Juan and I together while I was making love to my wife.

Later that year Tara went in for her annual check-up and the doctor discovered she had genital warts. Man it almost killed me watching the pain I put her through when the doctor had to put acid on them to get rid of them. When she had asked the doctor how she could have possibly contracted them. He told her you could only get them through having multiple sex partners. So we came home and she very respectfully asked me if I had been unfaithful to her. I looked her square in the face and out-in-out lied to this beautiful, precious woman that God had blessed me with. "Oh, man." I said to myself, "I'm no different than any of those homosexuals. God I hate myself!" But then reasoned,

"I just can't tell Tara the truth, she wouldn't understand. I don't think we've been married long enough for our relationship to withstand this kind of crisis. It's too vulnerable right now. I couldn't risk it. I'm glad Juan wanted to stop after all." I felt so guilty as I watched Tara on the doctor's table for yet another treatment to rid herself of the sexually transmitted disease I passed on to her. I watched a tear run down her innocent face from the pain she had to endure and the humiliation that went with being there. I was cut to the heart... but not for long.

Looking Out for #1 Continues and Spreads

Five months after Juan and I stopped, we picked up where we left off. I knew all too well about the sex drive of a teenage male. I'd been down that road many years earlier. That's why I wasn't too upset when Juan told me, "No more." I had kept just far enough away letting him have his space, but I would still show up at his house and visit with my extended family. I didn't treat Juan any differently than I treated his other brothers. I was still listening to his problems and offering advice. I was still the understanding one. I still talked to him with my arm around him, and gave him a gentle touch or nudge every now and then. That was my sign to make him aware that if he ever wanted to start up again, I was ready. Juan continued to be the family scapegoat, even though he tried so hard to be responsible. As his older twin, brothers began to work more hours at their after school and weekend jobs, their chores, and stuff around the house shifted to Juan. Therefore, Juan continued to feel used and abused. He doubted if his efforts were really worth being good. So eventually, he went back to what brought him comfort and escape from his problems, even if it was only a temporary fix.

We were back at our same routine. Getting together every chance, I could sneak him away into an empty room or out in the garage. Even though I was able to get Juan to resume our "relationship," he had developed a conscience, and was not always willing to get together when I came around. I grew tired of his fickle on again off again conscience. I thought, "You know this really stinks. Here I go to great lengths to spy out time to get together and Juan gets a conscience whenever HE feels like it." I felt frustrated and powerless. That was when I introduced Juan's stepbrother into my sick and perverted ways. Roberto was thirteen then. His barriers were already down because there were always plenty of hugs and wrestling to go around. I groomed and conditioned him much as I did with his older brother. We went camping and I set up the same scenario. As Roberto lay there half-asleep, I slowly started to massage him. I did exactly as I had done to Juan when I masturbated him for the first time a year and a half earlier.

Roberto was totally awake by the time he climaxed. As he was coming down from the new rush of feelings shooting through his body, I could see by the look on his face, he was terrified. "What in God's name are you doing?" was the look. However, he said,

"Why did you touch me and do that to me for?" He asked me with a quiver in his voice.

"I don't know" I stammered, "I'm sorry, very sorry. Please don't be mad at me, please. I'm sorry." He got up and left the tent, then went to sleep in their minivan. I was so stressed after that, I worried all night. I thought, "Oh, man, I really goofed this time. I am sooo dead!" I was only concerned with myself and about getting caught. The next day I was Roberto's best buddy. I kept apologizing and I felt like crap because I had violated another child. But, I knew that all of the "sorry's" in the world couldn't turn back time and undo the damage I had already done.

On the way home, Roberto sat in the very back of the van looking out the rear window. I took my own car and was following close behind them. All the way home he stared back at me as if to make sense of happened the night before. I'm sure he was wondering, "Who is that man my parents trusted enough as a friend and became a part of our family." That day, even though the sun was shining bright, it was a dark day as I saw the sparkle of childhood innocence drain from Roberto's eye. He never did tell on me and I sweated for two weeks over the prospects of my charades being exposed.

-CHAPTER FIFTY-

And the Masks Come Tumbling Down

Earlier in this book I made mention of my clowning business. Even after I moved to Kansas, I still did the clowning to make extra money from time to time. One of the last times I molested Juan was during a festival weekend that our town has every year. The community comes alive with local folks setting up booths and selling arts and crafts. They also have a big parade. That year I decided it would be fun to dress up in my clown outfit and be a part of the festivities. I put on a pair of stilts that made me a twelve-foot tall clown. I even made the local paper. I decided I needed an assistant during the weekend since Tara was running a craft booth, I arranged for Juan to help me. So we got ready for the parade. Even though Juan was sixteen, he thought it would be fun to be a clown too. So I dressed him up in a spare costume and we had a great time. After the parade, Juan and I went back to my house to freshen up. His father was picking him up that afternoon at the house and I needed to head back to the craft show to help Tara. But, before leaving the house, Juan and I masturbated together and during the middle of it, my thoughts started freaking out. "Oh, my God!" I thought to myself, "I am no different than those perverts you read about in the newspaper. The ones that dress up like Santa Claus or a clown and molest children. I am truly a sick, low life, scum of the earth." But, then

I thought, "No, this is different, because I have a relationship with Juan, I'm not traumatizing him. He likes this and knows that I love him." As I got ready to head out the door, I told him he did a great job at the parade and asked if he had a good time. He said,

"Yes, I had a really cool time. Thanks for letting me stay the weekend." I felt better after he said that, less guilty. "See, all is well." I tried to convince myself, yet I still felt lower than worm food.

Shortly after that, Juan and Roberto, his stepbrother were getting into a lot of trouble at home, and were spending a good amount of time being grounded to their room so they spent a lot of that time talking. Roberto told Juan that I showed him how to masturbate and Juan explained that I had showed him too. I knew this because of a question Roberto raised after the last time I molested him. I was massaging and arousing him while he was awake and he let me masturbate him. After that, I took his hand to have him touch my penis and Roberto jerked away then asked me,

"Why did you touch us and show us how to masturbate?" My reply was what I used to rationalize the whole way through molesting my half sister and my stepbrother when I was an adolescent. Then again, when I gave my ex brother-in-law a massage and touched him inappropriately. It was the same lame excuse, but it was the first time I heard it out loud and it didn't sound convincing to me either. Filled with shame, I told him,

"It happened to me when I was your age… my uncle showed me how." I could no longer keep eye contact with Roberto as I continued, "It helped me deal with my adolescent tumultuous times better." (I knew *that* was a blatant lie.) "So I thought I'd show you boys, too." I thought to continue by saying, "Because I love you guys so much." But, knew better to stop while I was still barely ahead, I felt completely ashamed of myself. As I finished my explanation, I thought, "Man, that is such a piss poor excuse and you know it. You're a straight up pervert." Roberto must have been reading my mind, because he wasn't buying into my reply either, and from that day forward, he stayed his distance away from me. Out of confusion and fear, Roberto kept my actions and my response to himself as long as he could.

Then at the end of that summer, I asked to have the boys stay the weekend at my house. Tara and I were going to have a garage sale and I called the boys' parents to see if I could get Juan and Roberto to help. They said it was okay and hung up. They told the boys what was going to take place and Roberto stressed out and said he didn't want to go over to our house. Then with a little prodding, he broke down crying and told his father everything. "I'm not lying, dad." He said, "You can ask Juan, he'll tell you too!" Juan concurred that what Roberto had said was in fact the truth …and good for him to have such courage and bravery. I even told him so in an apology letter I wrote to the Mendoza family shortly after my crime was exposed.

The next day, Raphael and Angelique asked me to meet at a local park so we could talk alone. I thought, "Okay, they want to talk to me. I wonder if the boys messed up and can't come." I wondered why they wanted to meet me at the park, but thought, "That's odd, but hey, anything they want is fine with me as long as I get the boys." I was curious as to our meeting, but confident that everything was going my way.

As we talked, they asked me what I had been doing to the boys. I instantly felt my little invincible, deceptive world slowly crumble to the ground. I did not deny anything but I didn't volunteer any information either, because I wasn't sure how much Juan had told them. I told Raphael and Angelica that I was sorry, but I was still worried about my own hide. I wasn't about to hang my own neck. I only confessed to what the boys had told them and I asked,

"Is there any way we can work this out just between us, you know, between you two and me?"

"Well, Jim, don't you think Tara deserves to know?" They asked

"Yes, yes, you're right. I'll tell Tara. The Masks were falling everywhere and I couldn't seem to catch them fast enough. They were crashing and disintegrating all around me. I felt embarrassed, exposed, and naked. I could hear them asking me,

"Why! Why would you do such a terrible thing to our children?" I told them the same thing I told Roberto a few months earlier. It didn't work then, but I didn't have a better explanation. I heard myself say defensively,

"I was a victim of child abuse when I was growing up, too!"

As I drove home to tell my wife what had happened that afternoon at the park, I felt humiliated, embarrassed and a victim of my own past. I thought, "Woe is me!"

-CHAPTER FIFTY ONE-

Suicide Attempt Number Three

After that day, I sank into the depths of despair. I stopped eating and I had not slept well in weeks. One day I decided to take all of my wife's anti-depressants. It was the strongest drugs in the house besides aspirin and I was not going to go down *that* road again, but still nothing much happened to me when I took them. Oh sure, I paid homage to the porcelain god again, however they put me in a catatonic state of mind. Tara was beside herself so I finally told her what I'd done and she made an appointment for me to see the psychologist. He recommended I check into a hospital psychiatric ward. I was there for a few days and I was encouraged when a friend called me to see how I was faring. I finally realized that I was not a god, but rather like a sinful human in need of therapy. After I hung up the phone, I felt loved. "Okay, Jimbo, you can do this." I thought to myself, "You've made some terrible mistakes, but this is a good time and place to start over with a clean slate. No more lies, no more Masks. You just need to get better; you've been sick for thirty-three years. You're not going to get well over night."

-CHAPTER FIFTY TWO-

No Regrets

After some deep, honest gut communication, Tara decided that she was going to stay and weather the storm with me. Tara saw that I was slowly realizing just how serious my deviant actions were, and how truly sorry I was for those actions.

We talked at length about her decision. I asked her if she could stay without having regrets later on down the line when things got tough. I knew I was in no position to give stipulations, but her decision was going to affect the both of us for the rest of our lives.

I told her about my first wife. How Alison had regrets, and threw them in my face. For nine years I heard, "I regret ever marrying you." Or, "I regret moving to California," and "I regret getting pregnant by you in the first place... I regret, I regret..." It was so hurtful and demoralizing to hear that continuously, even when I was trying to change for the better. We agreed that living with regrets was not truly living and that it wouldn't be fair to either of us if we had to live under those conditions.

I was honestly making changes like I promised her I would. I had regular visits with a psychologist and a psychiatrist who put me on medication.

During one of my visits with the psychologists, he told me that he would have to make a formal report about what I had done to the boys. The division of family services was finally notified, and then a police investigation finally ensued. That was nine months after the boys had first told their parents what I'd been doing to them.

-CHAPTER FIFTY THREE-

Getting What I Deserved

Later that week a police detective called and set up an appointment for me to come in at 8 a.m. on a Friday. I showed up at 7:30 AM, ready to spill my guts and come clean. The detective asked me,

"Are you sure you don't want your lawyer here, Mr. Petra?"

"Yes, I'm sure." I said. "I've already talked to him and he doesn't want me to talk. He also wants me to deny everything, sir." I told him, "I can't do that. I don't want to cause any more problems for this family or anyone else. I know my lawyer is going to be upset with me, but I truly want this monkey off my back and I want to get the proper help I need to stop this cycle of abuse." I told him that as the video camera was rolling. It felt good to come clean. It was such a relief. I thought, "You know, if I cooperate fully, maybe I'll just get a slap on the wrist and not have to do much jail time. I don't care if I'll have to register as a sex offender; at least I get the help I need."

(Every admission we make, and every secret we tell during our recovery will reflect who and where we are now. Telling our secrets helps us give them up. Asking for help acknowledges our need for others and helps us let go of the past.)

I was thirty-three years old when I was convicted of my crimes.

I was sentenced in two counties, the county where the boys lived, and the county where Tara and I lived. I was first prosecuted in my county court system. The night I was sentenced and locked up, I called Tara to see how she was holding up. There was a line of inmates and a time limit on the phone. It was very difficult for both of us, as we talked on the phone; we tried consoling each other to hang in there. Before we knew it, our time was up. As I said my goodbyes, Tara started to cry and beg to talk longer. Her heart was breaking. After we were cut off, I hung up the phone and went to my small cold grey cell where I cried and prayed. "Oh my God...what have I done? I have hurt so many people. I am so sorry. Please take care of my princess and give her the strength to get through this, and please be with the boys and their family, too. I am so sorry for what I've done. Please, oh please, forgive me." After I said Amen, I felt like the walls were closing in all around me, and rightly so.

Almost a month later, I was transferred to the county jail where the boys lived. It was election time and a new District Attorney was voted in and needed some time to become organized. So I stayed in the county jail for three months while I waited to be sentenced.

They were doing some remodeling work to the interior of the eighteen-man jailhouse. They found out I painted for a living and asked me if I wanted to paint. I was happy to get out of my cell and jumped at the chance to move around and stay busy. So for three weeks I put in ten to twelve hour days cleaning, prepping, painting, and cleaning up. With that kind of hard work plus taking prescription meds for my nerves and insomnia, I truly had no trouble falling asleep at night.

One of the jailers, who was about my age, used to be the town's trash collector for many years before his current occupation. This was his first year as a jailer, and he was working his way to becoming a police officer in a few months. One day, the old trash collector was pulling a double shift, swing, and graveyard. I was painting up front where the offices were. He was busy with some paperwork and his door was open. I was painting in the hallway. We were having a light conversation about nothing in particular. As he was filing papers and without looking up, he asked me if I liked what I was doing. I told him,

"Like is not the word, I *love* painting." Then his reply to what I said totally shocked me.

"Do you love it as much as sex?" he asked. I gasped at the words he just said.

"Well, of course not." I stammered with a little nervous chuckle. "Where did that come from?" I thought. He never did look up, and I continued to paint. Then around 9:00 pm, I finished cleaning up my tools and stopped for the day. I was tired and my muscles ached but I felt good about my accomplishments. Everyone was back in their cells and settling down for the evening.

It was time for the jailer to pass out bedtime meds. I was sharing a two-man pod with an old man. We each had our own little sleeping quarters and shared a table area plus bathroom. I had just showered and washed all my clothes and hung them up so I could wear them the next day. I had my yellow jumpsuit on and I was sitting on the floor, my cell mate was sitting at the small table. Both of us were watching television when the jailer came in with our meds. He came in and my cellie was busy asking him questions. As the jailer was facing us and talking, I noticed he was looking at me. Not at my face, but down at my lap. His eyes were fixed for the longest time. I looked down and noticed that my jumpsuit was unzipped, exposing my pubic area. I looked up and he was still gazing. I felt embarrassed, humiliated, and vulnerable. I sat there squirming for what seemed like an hour, when in reality, the jailer was only with us for less than five minutes and then he was gone.

After he left, I shrugged the whole thing off. "It must have all in my head? I'm reading way too much into things." I quickly forgot about it and finished watching the news. We were waiting for our drugs to kick in. We both took stuff to calm our nerves and help us sleep better. At about 10:15 pm we turned in for the night. In my sleeping quarters, I got out of my jumpsuit and put on a pair of shorts. It wasn't long before my meds kicked in and after working an eleven-hour day, I was out.

Sometime during the night, I was in a dream like state of mind. It felt just like I was with Juan having oral sex. It felt good, but I know I didn't climax. I was extremely groggy as I laid there on my back, then I turned over and faced the wall. That's all I remember.

In the morning, I woke up still facing the wall. I noticed my underwear was down below my knees and around my ankles. "That's odd." I said to myself. Then when I moved, I had this severe pain in my rear end. I had no idea what I'd done the day before to make me feel that bad. I went to the bathroom and I couldn't go. It felt like the worse case of constipation you could ever imagine. I took the day off because I wasn't feeling well.

That afternoon, I finally relaxed enough back there to relieve myself and when I did there was a discharge; it was semen. I was in a state of shock. I was scared, confused and in a state of panic. I couldn't tell anything to anyone. The very people my life depended on were in charge of me. I thought, "If I come forward with a rape accusation against a guard, I'd be in a real mess." Besides, it wasn't until I left the county jail that I pieced everything together.

I knew the other inmate didn't rape me, because our relationship never changed, besides the old man was very sickly and barely got out of his bed. I reflected back to that evening and how the jailer was acting, then when I saw him one last time before I transferred out to the 'Big House', I remembered he always avoided eye contact with me when we were talking.

Before that night, I knew my crime was widely known because it was printed on the front page of our small local paper, and the jailers had access to any files. The old trash man knew I had molested the teenage boys because I was charged with statutory sodomy. He must have thought I was into anal sex, so on that particular night he helped himself to a heavily sedated and tired sex offender. He probably said something like, "Hey, this is what to expect where you're heading…!" Who would they believe anyway?

~

I read somewhere that: "Sometimes it takes a major tragedy in order to come out of denial. Ironic, isn't it? One tragedy puts us in denial and another takes us out of denial." If I ever needed to stop and take inventory of my life, now was the time to start shedding the Masks. I did a lot of soul searching after being raped in the county jail. At first, I concluded that I deserved what I got because I felt lower than slug food about myself. Given enough time, a person can learn from every tragedy, given enough time… I learned from an adult's view what it was like to be a victim, trapped, scared, and vulnerable. A victim of someone in authority who held my life in their hands. That made me feel powerless, naked, and ashamed.

Many people may feel that they deserved to be abused. Whether you're a child or adult. Whether the abuse is physical, emotional, or sexual, bottom line is no one deserves to be abused!

It would be warped and sick to think I was blessed that it happened to me, not that any of my victims would mind, but I'm thankful I learned from that tragedy. If only I could express the depths of my sorrow and regret to all of the innocent people I victimized in my past. Of course. I could fill pages of useless: Shoulda, Woulda, and

Coulda's. However, victims don't want to hear excuses. They want and deserve action. So with 'Part Two' of this book, I would like to share with you what I've learned and has helped me to be successful in letting go of the many destructive, fake, and isolating Masks. *NOW* is the time to heal!

~

"No more masks means no more secrets,

no more secrets means no more victims."

PART TWO

~

...IN TIME WE HEAL."

"THOUGH NO ONE CAN GO BACK AND MAKE A
BRAND NEW START MY FRIEND, ANYONE CAN
START FROM NOW AND MAKE A BRAND NEW END."

\

"ABUSE BEGETS ABUSE"

From the book 'By Silence Betrayed', author John Crewdson: *"Because not all child sexual abusers were sexually abused as children, to say that the majority of adults who abuse children sexually were sexually abused themselves does not fully explain the root cause of child sexual abuse. When physical and emotional abuses are added to the equation; however, a common theme begins to emerge. Whether they were sexually abused, or beaten, or merely made to feel worthless, nearly all adults who have been caught having sex with children were badly mistreated by somebody when they were children. The answer, as simple as it is complex, appears to be, abuse begets abuse.*

~

What we live with we learn. What we practice we become. What we become has consequences. What we practice long enough becomes a cycle it becomes normal. Cycles are never questioned until they come to our attention. Cycles keep creating the same results, are they helping or hurting us?

~

Every admission we make and every secret we tell during our recovery will reflect who and where we are at the moment. Telling our secrets helps us give them up. Asking for help acknowledges our need for others and helps us let go of the past.

I'm reminded of an affirmation that's right on the mark for being successful at breaking the cycle of abuse:

"God did not give us a burning bush,

he gave us people to help us through life's journey."

This was the reason I named Part Two of this book

'In Time <u>We</u> Heal'.

-CHAPTER FIFTY FOUR-

We're ALL in This Together

I finally reached a point in my life where there was no place to go but up. It was time to stop and take a personal inventory of what I needed to do, then start changing. It was obvious to me that what I'd been doing all my life was not truly living, but merely surviving and thus far I hadn't done a great job at that either.

That's when I met Mary, a wonderful sweet woman, who had written a couple of inspiring stories for the book series 'Chicken Soup for the---Soul'. She volunteered her time and started a Friday morning twelve step self-help group. That humble, dear woman started me on a practical road to my trauma healing. In her self-help group, she told us:

"There are no shortcuts to any place worth going." She also taught us about the value of keeping a journal. She helped us realize the need to replace our self-condemning thoughts with positive affirmations. But, the most important thing she gave us was a safe place to go and share our wounded selves. The main rule that she stressed:

"What is said here, stays here." What was so wonderful about the group was it wasn't one big pity party session. It focused on healing properly and we couldn't do it successfully by ourselves. She and Delbert, who was her assistant, were not judgmental. They were human, with imperfections too. They made us feel that we were *all on the same healing path* that followed a twelve-step format adopted from Alcoholics Anonymous. We all listened, laughed, and cried together. By the time the morning was over, our hearts and inner batteries were filled and recharged. Those sessions allowed us to make it through yet another week, one day at a time, one moment at a time. They were beautiful people indeed.

I learned that journaling is vital because it forces you to express your self-destructive thoughts and feelings into words instead of just stomach churnings. Journaling can stop that broken record from playing deep inside. It allows you to acknowledge those thoughts that have been packed and stuffed into the corners of your brain, and release them to the page. This frees up your mind to replace negative destructive thoughts with the much needed positive thoughts and affirmations. Over the years, I have collected hundreds of positive, inspiring little stories and affirmations. Here are just a few that have helped me down the road to healing within:

*"A happy person is not one with a certain set of circumstances; but rather a person with a certain set of attitudes."

*"There is no better than here!"

*"The grass is *not* greener on the other side. It's greener where you water it more."

*"Not knowing who we are, we cling to others."

*"Knowing myself is the first step to accepting and loving myself."

*"My wounds from the past do not have to be fully healed
in order for me to start anew."

*"Change your thoughts and you change your world."

*"What am I saying to myself right now?

*"Don't believe everything you think!"

*"I will talk to myself in the same caring way I want others to talk to me."

*"I want to strive with all my heart to be myself. I don't need to pretend to be someone else now that I am becoming content with being me."

*"You can talk about how to change until the cows come home; but, until you decide to change, actively change, it is only then when you will stop your deviant cycle."

*"Unless you take full responsibility for your thoughts, feelings and actions, you will falsely believe that you have no control over yourself or your situation. You will feel, and seemingly become powerless."

*"Anyone can get angry—that is easy; but, to be angry with the right person, and to the right degree, and at the right time, and for the right purpose, and in the right way—that is not easy."

*"I've learned that I can't take away the past hurts I've caused, but I CAN change the way I treat others today."

*"Stop being sarcastic: sarcasm is like the tearing of flesh. It's worse than a cut with a knife. A knife makes a clean slice. A tear takes longer to heal and leaves a deeper scar."

Then from a book I read, about 'Forgiving our Shadows':

*"The worst prison for our minds is a dank, dark hole of misery, is a feeling of unworthiness, of self-anger or self hatred. 'Bad' people don't go to hell; they are already in hell, that's why they act so badly. I deeply believe that people can't cause more suffering than they themselves already feel inside. Disturbed people end up disturbing others."

I also learned something else in my Friday morning self-help group:

*"When you say 'I can't...' it keeps you a victim of whatever you *think* you can't do. Instead, say 'I won't right now, at this

point in my recovery, because I'm not ready yet.'----- You *do* have a choice, and that gives you the needed power to succeed at your own pace. Saying 'I can't!' keeps us stuck and feeling defeated.

We *can* do anything when the time is right."

*"Anger is a secondary emotion or feeling. For instance, a person experiences hurt or resentment first then usually reacts by becoming angry. When you are angry, then look closely at fear. When you see me angry ask, what am I afraid of? I might be afraid of being taken advantage of, or maybe being taken for granted, or not being taken seriously or I might be afraid of not measuring up to my own expectations."

*"It is better to <u>explain</u> your anger, then to express it. It's easy to express your anger, people can easily see you're mad, however if you <u>explain</u> your anger, you give people the chance to understand you."

*"*Any* change, even a change for the better, is always accompanied by some discomfort."

*"Don't let your weaknesses overshadow your strengths. Choose allies stronger than your weaknesses."

What are some affirmations that you have found profound or inspiring to you? _____

_____

_____

_____

_____

_____

_____

_____

Talking One to One

Trauma healing groups are great but even if you can get together with one other adult child of abuse, it can prove to be healing. Like the time I was out walking with my friend Allen one afternoon. Allen said to me, "I believe we are made up in four parts:
Our Conscience:

1.) The desire to do what is good and right.

2.) Our Dysfunction; the "Evil" or sinful survival skills we have.

3.) Our Child within; or our gut feelings and intuition.

4.) Our Adult self; the part that helps to re-parent our inner child.

Then Allen asked me, "Jimbo, how do I block out "Evil" so that it'll be safe for my Child within to come out?"

"To try to totally block out Evil." I explained to him, "That would be next to impossible because we are all imperfect. However, to be *aware* of "Evil" is to keep it in its place. Just like a real child, you cannot shelter it forever from bad things happening to them. That would not only be impossible but also not fair for their balanced growth. We *can* however hold their hand and be there like a loving and supportive parent would be in times of crisis. Not like we were treated while growing up." Then he told me, "I want to give my inner child love. Give it the love that the eight year old needed when they came and took my parents away."

"Do you think you had been shown, proper nurturing and secure love before that time?" I asked him and continued, "Did you truly know what love was then and is now? Do you know what balanced, respectful boundaries were and are now? Do you know what secure love is now, so you can give it to your inner child?"

Through our conversation, he realized that as children, we were clueless. But that as adults we're learning about it now so we can continue to heal and grow. We need to strive to re-parent ourselves. We need to allow our inner child to use the power it already has, but is afraid to use. Our inner child needs to start listening and trusting those gut feelings or intuition instead of relying on our dysfunctional survival skills, be they "Evil" or not. Then our inner child can truly work hand in hand with our adult self to restore our good conscience, which was stolen from us as children.

Trauma healing and recovering addicts of any kind are experts in what doesn't work in a family environment. We have learned that it's never too late to get unstuck and start over again. We just have to use better tools and guidelines, with the hope of succeeding in having a happy family life as opportunities present themselves again.

From the book 'If Only My Family Understood Me...' by Don Wegscheider. The, 'Signs of a Healthy Family' explains that each member has:

*The ability to Negotiate with other members of the family without put-downs.

*The ability to say yes or no without the price of rejection.

*The ability to ask without demanding.

*The confidence in the stability of the relationship.

*The ability to show feelings of all kinds without fear of losing the relationship.

*The ability to have specific relationships with individuals in the family.

*The confidence in the honesty of the family members, and feeling trusted by others.

*The ability to celebrate, have fun and play.

Respect for Boundaries

While in trauma healing, we've learned the true depth of our physical abuse and the torturous pain we endured as children resulting in a lack of boundaries of others.

During my dysfunctional childhood, boundaries were never properly identified. Instead, they were blurred and often violated. If they were explained at all, it was through shaming, blaming, and double standards.

Respect for boundaries is crucial to your own recovery. If we don't recognize our boundary issues then we will continue the cycle of abuse. We will tell ourselves "It happened to me, and I turned out just fine!" That, my friend, is the biggest and most destructive lie we can ever tell ourselves! A lie that keeps us stuck and sets us up to continue the cycle of abuse, no matter what kind.

We *must* become aware that *everyone* has a right to his or her own personal boundaries. We not only need to respect those boundaries, but we also need to realize that we too have personal boundaries that deserve respect. If we don't feel worthy enough to have people honor our own boundaries then we set ourselves up for thinking it must be okay to violate the boundaries of others.

For example, another treatment group member, named Carl, was telling me that he had to explain to his wife that he was not comfortable with her play biting while they made love. Carl had the courage to identify his personal boundaries to his wife. We cannot afford to be physically hurt for someone else's pleasure anymore. We don't need the flashbacks. We don't want to hurt anyone else again, and we do not want anyone to hurt us.

Can you reflect on some boundary issues that you have tolerated in the past, because you didn't want to make the other person upset, or you didn't feel worthy enough to speak up?

_____

_____

_____

_____

_____

_____

_____

_____

_____

_____

_____

_____

_____

_____

_____

_____

_____

_____

Please remember, *everyone* has the right to have their personal boundaries acknowledged and respected. Below is my personal bill of rights, yours may differ a little according to your own history and where you are in your own healing within process. I strongly encourage you to create your own personal 'Bill of Rights.'

MY PERSONAL BILL OF RIGHTS

I HAVE A RIGHT TO ACKNOWLEDGE AND GET TO KNOW MY CHILD WITHIN.

I HAVE A RIGHT TO I HAVE A MULTITUDE OF CHOICES IN MY LIFE BEYOND MERELY SURVIVAL.

I HAVE A RIGHT TO ALL OF MY FEELINGS AND TO EXPRESS THEM PROPERLY.

I HAVE A RIGHT TO CHANGE AND IMPROVE MYSELF.

I HAVE A RIGHT NOT TO JUSTIFY MYSELF TO OTHERS.

I HAVE A RIGHT TO MAKE KNOWN THE TRUTH ABOUT MY BOUNDARIES AND LIMITS.

I HAVE A RIGHT TO PUT MYSELF FIRST SOMETIMES.

I HAVE A RIGHT TO SAY "NO" AND BE OKAY ABOUT MY DECISION.

I HAVE A RIGHT TO NEED THINGS FROM OTHERS.

I HAVE A RIGHT TO MY OWN TIME AND SPACE REQUIREMENTS WITHOUT BEING MADE TO FEEL GUILTY ABOUT IT.

I HAVE A RIGHT TO BE OKAY WITH WHERE I'M AT IN TRAUMA HEALING.

I HAVE A RIGHT TO ASK FOR HELP, EMOTIONAL SUPPORT OR ANYTHING ELSE I NEED. (EVEN THOUGH I MAY NOT ALWAYS GET IT.)

I HAVE A RIGHT TO FORGIVE OTHERS.

I HAVE A RIGHT TO FORGIVE MYSELF.

I HAVE A RIGHT TO GRIEVE AND LET GO OF ALL THE BAD THINGS THAT HAPPENED TO ME.

I HAVE A RIGHT TO GRIEVE ABOUT WHAT I DID NOT RECEIVE.

I HAVE A RIGHT TO BE LISTENED TO AND UNDERSTOOD WITHOUT BEING CUT OFF IN MID SENTENCE.

I HAVE A RIGHT SOMETIMES, TO INCONVENIENCE OR DISAPPOINT OTHERS.

I HAVE A RIGHT TO LET OTHERS RESOLVE THEIR OWN DILEMMAS.

I HAVE A RIGHT TO COUNT ON OTHERS TO BE OPEN AND HONEST WITH ME AND ME WITH THEM.

I HAVE A RIGHT TO SELF RESPECT AND DIGNITY.

*IF I HAVE A RIGHT TO THE ABOVE-MENTIONED,
        THEN OTHERS HAVE THESE RIGHTS TOO.

-CHAPTER FIFTY FIVE-

"What's Your Reward?"

*A*s you have read this book, you have no doubt seen a number of thinking errors / patterns that led me to the poor choices I made. In my opinion, the most damaging thought pattern that puts us at a higher risk of re-offending or at least lapse in our treatment is that of poor self-esteem and feelings of worthlessness. After getting caught molesting the boys it seemed prophetic in a way. Now I was *officially* labeled a 'piece of crap', 'scum of the earth', which had always been my self-image. There seemed to be nowhere to go but up and at that time I didn't know how to do that. Even today, I have to remind myself that it took a lifetime to build these emotional brick walls. So the road of recovery was not going to be a quick patch job. It will mean a complete demolition of those walls. We must replace the self-destructive thoughts with healthy positive thoughts. This will make our recovery much easier and gives us a second chance to make everyone around us be and feel safer as we all go down life's road together. I had to realize every decision I make has some type of reward. If I change my behavior and do what is appropriate, my reward is a good conscience knowing that I'm on the right path. Now think about this, a decision doesn't always have to be an action. It can also be a thought. For instance, I've struggled with my anger and low self-esteem for as long as I can remember, and one day I was in a session with my treatment group and the therapist posed this question to me:

"What's your reward?" I must have looked as dumb founded as I felt inside because she repeated the question,

"What's your reward for hanging on to such destructive self talk as 'I'm a worthless, no good piece of crap' for all the bad loathsome things I've done in my life.' What do you get out of it?" she asked. I couldn't believe she was serious, how can anybody think that a person could benefit from such negative thoughts. I got so frustrated at her assuming that I was actually *gaining* something from staying stuck with my self-condemnation, that I couldn't answer her and she moved on to something else.

I stewed on her question all week long and then one night, about two in the morning it dawned on me that my reward was for thinking all that negative self talk; Even though it was driving me insane, I chose to stay in that dark mental place because, 1) I was comfortable and 2) I didn't have to challenge myself to change. Let's face it, change, even for the good, can be frightening. You see, thinking is a *choice* just like choosing not to offend again is a choice. I realized that it simply wasn't enough to decide not to do a particular behavior because it's wrong and my actions would affect many innocent people, that is extremely important but it's not enough. Decide to believe in our self and in the fact that "Yes we've made mistakes, maybe even horrific mistakes but we have to separate the deed from the doer." First, we must choose to change our thinking process. If we do not, and we choose to continue with our negative self-talk then we might as well be a ticking time bomb. Because eventually our thoughts will drag us down and sabotage our recovery.

Statistics show that there is a higher recidivism rate for sex offenders than any other crimes committed. That means that sex

220

offenders are more likely to reoffend then other crimes. One of the main reasons, I believe, is because sex offenders stay stuck in their self-destructive loathing. When fueled with outside stresses some have said,

"Screw it I can't do it. I'm just a piece of crap and always will be!" It is that kind of negative self-talk that gets us to stop applying ourselves in treatment. Our reward for such thinking, can lead us back to a prison cell for a very, very long time.

The attitude "What's the use in trying in the first place…" only serves a self-destructive course of action that led me to continue abusing. However,

'I've learned not to quit when the tide is lowest,

for it's just about to turn.'

I get so filled with disgust and self-hatred when I think of all the wicked and evil things I have done and the lives I've destroyed. Sometimes I have bad days where I wallow in my toxic guilt and shame. On those day's I make myself reach for my affirmation collection or read some 'Healing Within' books to help my thoughts get back on track. Sometimes, when I'm in that state of mind, it is hard to tell someone that I'm struggling because 'I'm a man and I can handle anything!' Then I remind myself, again, that some of my worst thinking contributed to some of the worst behaviors a person can do to another human being. So I do the truly manly thing and talk to someone, my wife and or dear friend when I find myself drowning in my own toxic cesspool of stinking thinking. They remind me that they don't see the same person I do. They see a man that, has made some mistakes, but has been working hard to change through recovery and is an equally hard working and kind husband and friend. It helps a lot to hear such words when the "voices" in my head tell me otherwise. Then I make the choice to stop my negative self talk and actively take positive steps to fill my mind with good affirmations that will help me continue with the best reward of all and that is, I'm worthy of staying victim free, and so are you.

"I can't climb up hill if I have down hill thoughts."

-CHAPTER FIFTY SIX-

Still Much to Learn

*J*ournal entry November 11, 3:10 a.m.

(Man I hate being plagued by insomnia!)

I read in a book recently about abused boys that when they grow up they can be so far in denial of the pain they've suffered and their own feelings, that they have a decreased ability to be empathizing with others. I recall an experience before I married my first wife; I was visiting with Alison's mother in their living room while Alison was in the kitchen making refreshments for us. She was getting some ice cubes for our drinks when all of a sudden she belted out a blood-curdling scream of pain. As she was opening the freezer, a package of frozen vegetables fell on her bare feet. I don't recall what was going through my mind but I didn't even react to her cry. Alison's mother, Rosemary called out,

"Are you okay?" Then looked at me dumfounded and said,

"Get in there and see if she's all right for crying out loud!"

"Oh yeah…Okay." I replied as I got up reeling from Rosemary's rebuke. I have always had a problem with being numb to other people's physical pain. Through the years, however, my response has improved in emergencies. Once Alison and I were vacationing with another couple and their little boy, the child was injured while jumping on the hotel room bed. While everyone else was in hysterics, I was able to calmly take care of the situation and get everyone to the emergency room where he received four stitches. I thought to myself that I could perhaps make a good paramedic if it wasn't for the queasiness I experience at the very sight of blood and guts.

Now that I am to a point in my trauma healing where my own internal wounds have been exposed I find that I can more readily acknowledge my own feelings and those of others. I am able to show more empathy towards those in physical and emotional pain, as many times people just want you to listen and to be there for them, to feel the pain with them.

Have you experienced something similar because of what you lived through? _____

_____

_____

_____

_____

_____

_____

_____

_____

_____

_____

The most important lesson learned on my journey of self-healing:
EMPATHY: HAVING THE ABILITY TO PUT MYSELF IN SOMEONE ELSE'S SHOES AND REALIZING THAT *EVERYTHING* I DO AND SAY WILL AFFECT OTHERS FOR THE GOOD OR THE BAD.

Before I came to the above conclusion, I had to first journey back to heal my child within teaching myself deeper empathy.

The poem sighted below is by Laura Donaforta from her Book 'I Remembered Myself:' I couldn't think of a more fitting way to acknowledge my own child within because she talks about the acknowledgement of her child within after surviving childhood sexual abuse. She gave permission to use this in my book and to change the gender.

"To Me"

"Little boy, I'm sorry.

Brave little one, I'd like to make it better,

Of course, I wish I'd been there,

Of course, I wish I'd never left you.

Free to be so vulnerable.

Of course, I wish,

But then…

It's happened, and you are still

A little boy and I'm your dad.

Though I were with you

Pain would yet have been your path,

And you would yet have been vulnerable,

Though not so free.

And dear little one,

Now you're crying.

Are you frightened still?

You've made it though

My friend, you were strong,

But now let go.

Come here, I'll carry you awhile.

Little ones shouldn't have to be strong.

Poor baby, I'll hold you.

As if my loving hands would

Recreate the child who could trust.

But yet betrayal,

Pain,

Fear,

Anger and shame

Would someday break upon you

So if it must be now, I'm sorry, love.

I'd stop it if I could

But let me give you what I can

Though I cannot hide you,

I will hold you.

Though I cannot make your suffering easy,

I will lend and teach you strength.

I will love you, my little child within."

Once I started to take care of my child within, I then was able to have empathy for other people. Once I stopped denying my own pain, I stopped denying the pain I put others through all my life. Hurting people hurt people, and I want to continue to learn and to let go of my inner pain so I can stop being a pain.

What are some kind words you would like to say to your child within? Maybe find a tissue box and poor out your heart.

Dear Child Within,

_____

_____

_____

_____

_____

_____

_____

Once I realized that I was worthy of my own "personal bill of rights" then that gave me the inner power I needed to live without abusing others by taking their rights away. Another key to stopping the cycle of abuse is to remember we're always worthy enough to take control of our own future actions by actively working on our healing process. Just like acknowledging others having a 'Personal Bill of Rights', so too, they are worthy of not being abused any longer.

They are worth it, because I am worth it, and you are too.

"They're worth it, because I'm worth it."

I started a recovery program and to change,

because I'm worth it.

I started to acknowledge my Child within,

because I'm worth it.

I worked hard to remember my thoughts and feelings of long ago,

because I'm worth it.

I worked hard to stop denying just how horrific I was treated and what I endured, because I'm worth it.

I continued to expose the many Masks that kept me stuck,

because I'm worth it.

I continued to learn what having empathy for myself involved,

because I'm worth it.

I finally saw just how devastatingly hurtful I was to others,

because they're worth it.

I finally stopped abusing others physically, emotionally and sexually,

because they're worth it.

I finally put away the hypocritical and isolating Masks,

because we're ALL worth it.

"More Things I've learned"

I've learned that people who behave as though they are God's gift to humanity are people with low self-esteem.

I've learned that when I choose to do something with an open heart I normally make the right decision.

I've learned that there is no pillow, softer than a clear conscience.

I've learned that comparing myself to others is fruitless. As they have not been where I have, nor experienced the exact same thing that I have.

I've learned that God didn't do it all in one day. What makes me think I can?

I've learned that when life makes me feel like my chest is in a vice as my breathing becomes tense, I usually have inside tears that are demanding to be outside tears.

I've learned that when I am battling with inner demons alone, somewhere deep inside, I know that I am rejecting the presence of God

I've learned that even if I am experiencing "pain," I don't have to be a "pain."

I've learned that it's okay for two people to look at the same thing and yet view it totally different.

I've learned that if I am always a pillar to my friends, I will feel lost and lonely during the times I need them the most.

I've learned that families are not necessarily biological.

I've learned that no matter how good a close relationship is, people or individuals are going to hurt me sometimes and I must forgive them for that.

I've learned that more often than not, a change of self is required more than a change of surroundings.

I've learned that when I ignore the facts it does not change the facts.

I've learned that no matter what the results are, if I am honest with myself, I will succeed.

I've learned that working on myself is worth it.

I've learned to release negative, unproductive emotions that come from anger, in a positive, productive way.

I've learned the purpose of Satan and all his wicked forces is to take away one's self worth.

I've learned I do have great value.

I've learned that sometimes love and life gives you a second chance.

I've learned that I still have a lot to learn.

What have you learned so far in your trauma healing or recovery? _____

_____

_____

_____

_____

_____

_____

_____

_____

_____

_____

_____

_____

_____

_____

_____

_____

_____

-CHAPTER FIFTY SEVEN-

Writing Down the Bones

*F*or the past few years now, I've kept a journal. Sometimes I write in it daily and then at other times I try to write in it at least once a week. I've collected newspaper clippings, magazine articles, and hundreds of copied pages from books. These things have helped me deal with various issues that I have to work through. So far, my journal weighs about ten pounds. When it gets to be over four inches thick, I clean it out and start again.

Once Upon a Time Until You're Ready

Someone in my 12-step group mentioned that they started to write out their own experiences of child abuse in their journal. I thought it was an excellent idea, and that's how I got started. I found it very difficult to start writing my own history because I didn't know where to begin opening up all of those hidden festering wounds. I was encouraged to first just write the event down on paper and if that was still too difficult then to pretend I'm telling a story about someone else, thus taking myself totally out of the situation. So that's what I did, I began to listen to my child within and I even gave him his own name. Then soon all of these stories started to unfold from deep within the caverns of my wounded self. I started with the minor ones, and as I regained more self-awareness and understanding, I dove down deeper to unearth the more heinous abuse.

It was a long journey; I was to learn that it was not going to get better until it seemed to get worse first. Months later, I was able to go back through my stories and put the much needed thoughts and feelings into those experiences. Then eventually I wrote in the real names of all those who treated me so poorly, by doing so it helped me put the responsibilities back on the proper shoulders of where it belonged. It was only then did I cease in carrying the entire world on my own. I finally put my own name into the stories so I could see just how much damage I had caused in abusing others, thus taking the rightful ownership of my own actions.

By going back and recalling the situations that led up to a certain event(s), helped me to make better sense of the choices I made. Like for instance when I was thirteen and attempted to kill myself. For years, I couldn't figure out why I would do such a thing. But by going back further that year, I was able to see that there were numerous events, that led up to that day.

And when I molested my little half sister. Again, another question: What possessed me to do that? Equating sex with love and just plain choosing to continue being sneaky like we were when Uncle Everett molested all of us, and enjoying the feelings it made me feel. By writing all this out, I was able to learn that all of the events in my life have explanation to the many unanswered questions that have plagued and kept me stuck in toxic shame and guilt for so long. All of those questions like, "Why did I do this?" or "What on earth was I thinking to allow myself to do that?" I'm not trying to justify my behavior by any means however, it does shed light on why I made those bad decisions. By learning to question your thoughts and your feelings before you act will help prevent you from continuing the cycle of abuse in the future.

Please, I encourage you to start writing your own story. As tough as it was reading through my life experience, can you at least relate to it a little bit? If you have gone through worse, let me tell you I'm sorry, you too have some hard work ahead of you my friend. If you feel better about yourself because at least you hadn't done......... that's okay too. If you have a trauma history, please *never* think it's any less horrific. It's your experience; nobody else was in your shoes. Nobody was there for you to protect you from harm. Stop minimizing what you went through. If you can begin to work through your trauma, you will better understand and stop minimizing the harm you might have done to others.

Healing in Numbers

While others in trauma healing benefit from hearing our history, the person who benefits the most is the teller. Hearing our own story unfold from the depths of our soul, from our child within, it is only then that we find out the truth about ourselves. It sets us free from the debilitating bondage of our toxic secrets. It loosens the suffocating grip that our dysfunctional masks have had on us.

I had moved to another town where I was blessed to meet this neat big-hearted bear of a man, Wayne Marlow who was a Psychologist. He had started a group session that to this day I am forever indebted to have been a participant. I am so thankful that they were there to listen to my pain. It was the very first place where I shared my 'Once upon a times' and they helped me turn them into 'I remember when...' stories. Here are a couple of journal entries from those first healing days.

May 23, 9:00 pm

"Today I read the story called 'An old expression becomes a reality.' When I shared this event with my Monday afternoon group, they all adamantly explained to me that what was done to me was NOT discipline; but in fact it was abuse and there is NOTHING a seven year old child could possibly ever do to merit such punishment... It felt good to hear this."

Oct. 8, 11:45 pm

"Today I read 'Ten year old Homo...' It took a tremendous amount of courage to, not only relive this but more importantly, to share it with my trauma healing group. This was the first time I was able to tell the complete account of what happened so many years ago.

While I was growing up, it was a constant battle to tell my side of the story. It didn't matter what kind of event took place; and this one, like everything else that happened in my life, was silenced and never dealt with again. It was stuffed down and hidden away.

It's no wonder I was sexually confused. I had been sexually exploited and abused by three different males. Unfortunately, those experiences molded me into the person I am today.

Why didn't red flags go up for my parents when their ten-year-old child experimented with sex in an attempt to gain acceptance, attention, and affection from a male teenager? What a thing for a child to be labeled a homosexual only to have the whole thing swept under the rug nice and neat like nothing ever happened.

I am so grateful to be able to have a safe place to share my past. It has helped in my healing. It is so liberating, and yet at the same time calming. I am no longer silenced I am blessed and will continue my healing journey of exposing my masks.

(End of journal entry.)

"Why Did You Pick Me As Your Victim?"

That is one of the questions, victims of sexual abuse often ask. There are as many answers to that question as there are many perpetrators. There are, however, similarities in most reasons why people choose to sexually abuse others, whether it is towards a child or an adult. One reason is sexual abuse often has nothing to do with sex at all. Most of this insidious behavior has to do with power and control issues. Perpetrators often lack control in their own lives, in addition to their improper problem solving skills. They attempt to put on a mask that, "Everything is *fine*" in their world, when in reality they know deep down inside, their world is a living hell. They lack the knowledge and skills or simply have too much pride to stop the insanity. Thus, a person acts out on another person and uses sex as the means to gain power and control over somebody else.

Why do some commit sex crimes against children? Bottom line is some adults are attracted to children; who are fresh, untouched, and innocent. They have developed improper sexual fantasies, which began simply with a thought and allowed to continue festering until some act on their fantasies, at which time; it no longer stays a thought but becomes a behavior. That is why it is imperative for an offender to seek help in changing their thought process and to do away with their sexual

234

fantasies that violate other people's boundaries. We must stop looking at others, whether they are adults or children, as mere objects of gratification. When we start respecting others, then the cycle of abuse will end. And then we will start respecting ourselves.

So to answer the above question personally was difficult. It took me a while to dig deep within me and come up with the truth. I'm not proud of the answer, but it shows where my mind was at the time of my offending:

I picked Juan because he was male, and there was no way he was going to get pregnant. Since I dreaded having my own offspring because I knew that I was truly scum of the earth and I was convinced that I could never be a good father. I thought, "I could never be a decent husband, let alone a worthy father." I felt worthless and ashamed of my entire existence.

I picked a child because I had anger and control issues. I knew if my wife ever withheld sex from me, then I had a convenient back up plan. Why didn't I just seek out a woman? At the time, I honestly thought, "That would be adultery. That would mean having sexual intercourse with another woman to get my needs met, and to get together with another man is out of the question, that would be so wrong if I went that route. Besides, the diseases that these people put themselves at risk for gives me the shivers just thinking about it. I needed to feel superior to those men. I thought, "This is different." What I was doing with Juan, "This is no big deal. It happened to me... nobody is getting hurt." That is how I rationalized things in my mind to justify my own sick actions.

There are times when victims of sexual abuse take the initiative in the sexual encounter with the perpetrator. I can't tell you how many times I've heard, "Well, he/she came on to me, what was I to do?" Sadly, there were times in the course of the two years when I was victimizing Juan that he approached me. That made me think that my actions were okay and that I wasn't hurting him after all. This reasoning of course was wrong. Children do not have the mental capacity to give consent, which is why there are laws protecting them from sexual abuse.

Some child victims of abuse are confused as to why they initiated sex even though they knew it was wrong. Then they later feel guilty for being a willing participant. Once again, we have to remember the main issue here is not about the sex act, it's about power and control. If the victim of sexual abuse knows the routine of their perpetrator and knows, the inevitable is going to take place. The victim will, at times, take control of the situation and simply get it over with just so that the perpetrator will leave them alone. This may give the victim a sense of power and control over the abuser.

-The Butterfly Effect-

We can start anywhere to improve the quality of life for the betterment of the human family. Have you ever heard of the Butterfly Effect? Sometime in the 1960s, a meteorologist ascertained that small, nearly indiscernible changes in weather could affect global weather patterns. He coined the phenomenon the 'Butterfly Effect' because, as he put it, a butterfly that flaps its wings in Brazil might create a tornado in Texas. So too, within the human race, the Butterfly Effect has been in action with us. For instance, a negative result of the Butterfly Effect in the case of my own upbringing;

> *Instead of the training that a mother does with her son. Gentle correction and discipline, it was severe beatings that left welts and bleeding…then physical scars.
> *Instead of the training that a father does with his son. Gentle words of wisdom backed with patience and kindly encouragement, it was critical speech and a deadly

disapproving glare from my father's eye that pierced the very soul of his child…then the emotional scars set in.

*Instead of the training that a neighbor, uncle and older 'friend' does with a child. Gentle hugs and caress' can quickly turn into inappropriate fondling and touching of each other's genitals…then confusion, guilt and toxic shame sets in with yet another isolating secret and the self concluding false fact that it is the child's own fault.

Thus, the negative impact of the Butterfly Effect on a child can start out as harmless and non-threatening as can be, then turn into a deadly F-5 tornado within the child and ultimately committing soul murder. Thus, very likely, passing on that training they received to others, and so continuing the cycle of abuse, even though they know it's wrong, but because of severe denial and poisonous pride. Change rarely takes place until the abuser is forced to come face to face with their own demons and learn to deal with them properly. However, just as change is a choice, the Butterfly Effect can also be applied to good, if we choose to. When we realize that one very small positive change in us can lead to another change then before long it starts to snowball into effecting others for the good too. This can happen anywhere at any time. We do not have to wait for others to make changes. We can get the ball rolling ourselves by taking the proper steps to stop the cycle of abuse today, right now! By sharing our stories and caustic secrets with others like I have. By exposing one mask at a time, it literally destroys their hold on us. Let the positive Butterfly Effect start with you.

-CHAPTER FIFTY EIGHT-

Letting Go and Reflect on Good Memories

*T*he shear evasiveness of the abuse when I was a child / teenager, and having to stuff and squelch all those feelings and experiences for so long, was like a death, where the sadness and anger are dealt with properly. With time, I've noticed just how powerful our emotional baggage can be. I learned to use that negative energy to my advantage in a positive way. Taking baby steps and convincing my inner child that it was okay to come out and express himself. Feeling so unworthy, I couldn't even stand to write "I" statements let alone read it in someone else's book. I hadn't realized I minimized my feelings so much. Then I began the grieving process, I went from sad and hurt, to anger. It was from *that* energy that I tapped into. To fuel my desire to plow head long into going deeper into exposing all of those dirty little secrets that had kept me so stuck and isolated for such a long time. I was angry with everyone who had anything to do with messing up my life, but then I began to get mad at myself because, "You're not supposed to get angry." I was taught that, "Anger is bad and wrong." but then I learned the truth. Anger is an emotion like all of the others, and it has its place in our feelings just like all the rest. Anger is *not* wicked and wrong, but it can be if used improperly. I have to remind myself from time to time, "*I* have emotions, *they* don't have me." I also needed to remember how to let all of those pent up emotions run their course.

It was all part of the grieving process. Grieving for a childhood that never was.

I also learned that it is okay if we don't want to forgive those who have wronged us… but what they don't tell you is that it comes with a price. Unresolved feelings of resentment keep us stuck! By harboring resentment for someone who has hurt us, allows that person to live rent free in our head. It continues to give them power over us. Now that I know that, I can't afford it and nobody is worth that today. Instead, I choose to be a responsible landlord of my mind and evict them; I won't allow hurtful squatters to stay there any longer.

*There are only two things a person, truly has control over,

     1) How I think

     2) How I act / react.

'The Power of Memories' by Frank Minirth states, "You cannot turn negative programming into positive programming. However, very frequently the negative messages in a person's memory overpower the positive ones…dig out the positive messages that run counter to the negative ones. Bringing them to light will do much toward helping you balance negative effects, and that is a key factor in altering bad memories." This is true whether we are working on building a more positive relationship in your marriage or working through childhood trauma.

I mentioned something back in Chapter Forty-One about working up the nerve to ask my mother why she treated me the way she did back when I was a child. Her reply was generally always the same,

"I'm sorry for all that but…" It has only been recently through my trauma healing that I've had to realize that no matter what her reply was, it would never undo the hurt and damage that was done. There would never be any magical words to make sense of any of it or make it all go away.

I have also learned that the one who benefits the most from an apology is the one saying it and not necessarily the one who was wronged. While it definitely helps to hear that, someone is truly sorry like I am towards the ones that I've abused. The simple truth of the matter is this:

All victims really want to know is

1) The perpetrator takes full responsibility

for their actions, and

2) Gets the proper help they need.

3) Stop abusing.

Mother never even made it off first base. Yes, she did say that she was sorry but then she'd start playing the blame game. I remember one of her favorite sayings; "It takes a big man to say he was wrong, and an even bigger man to say he's sorry." Mother lived by those words too. For instance, when one of her friends would call her on the carpet about something wrong she did or said she never had any problem admitting she was at fault and she'd readily apologize.

As I grew older, I started to doubt her sincerity at times. Sadly, I even learned from her that saying you're sorry can also be very easy for someone devious and manipulative to say when need be. Today though, is another story, I've realized that being sorry is more than just words it requires action. In order for me to continue my recovery and staying victim free, I had to stop blaming my abusive behavior on other people. As true as it is "I was abused therefore I abuse." The fact of the matter is there are a lot of victims of all kinds of childhood abuse that do not continue that cycle of abuse, yet instead may act out in their self destructive, addictive behaviors.

But there are ones who have been able to recognize the harm and devastation of such abuse and have taken positive steps to do two things, learn from others the correct way of rearing the next generation properly and were able to let go of their past by labeling it for what it really is, history.

For the ones who have passed on the abuse to the next generation, like myself, have some work to do, and it's never too late to make a better future/history for ourselves, and for the community. Our past has to be dealt with properly. After we do so then the next step is letting go and moving on. We can't move on if we keep dwelling on negative experiences and memories. Scars remind us of where we've been, but they don't have to dictate our future. As hard as it may seem, we need to dig down deep and try to recall some good memories however small they may be.

I recall some good experiences in my life, once a month my father would take the family out on the town. I fondly remember, he would have a twenty-dollar bill, take all five of us to an -all you can eat- restaurant, and later the dollar theater. We'd see a new movie on its last weeks at the box office but we didn't care, it was new to us. Those were the rare evenings that the Petra family seemed to leave all our problems at home for a few hours and take a much needed break and attempt to be a decent family after all.

I fondly recall Leslie had some of her happier days when she'd set aside a month or two each year to do volunteer work. The atmosphere at home seemed to be a little less poisonous during those weeks she spent more time helping others; it helped her to feel better about herself. In that aspect I am grateful to Leslie for being a good example of someone who reaps blessings if they stayed busy doing Good deeds. It was because of noticing those happier times she had that made me want to do some volunteer work myself.

I recall a person at the congregation that was pivotal in my positive growth. She started back during my tumultuous pre-teen years;

I must have been almost twelve at the time when this wonderful woman used to pull me aside and say positive things to me like how she enjoyed hearing me make a comment during the meeting or that the shirt and tie I wore looked good on me. I didn't know how to respond to receiving so very kind and nurturing words. My step-grandmother was standing beside me on one of those occasions while I stood there in a trance like state, my heart was like a thirsty sponge and was sucking it all in. As grandma gently nudged me and told me to say thank you, I came back down to earth and remembered my manners.

"Thank you." I said sheepishly. I didn't want her to stop; I could have stayed and listened for hours.

From time to time, she pulled me aside and fill my heart up again. Somehow, she knew just when I needed it the most. I will be forever indebted to her and she probably never knew the good she was doing. I'd like to think that she originated the affirmation;

"Praise a child and he will prosper."

And then there are those memories of my first hero, my older brother Jason, he taught me how to play baseball. And then there were also the hours we'd spend on the playground in the summertime running through the clover, catching honeybees, and putting them into jars. There was even a short period of time our mother took a break from beating us. She kept busy making refrigerator magnet art. She made things like little caterpillars out of pipe cleaners and felt, then glue on those cute little plastic eyes that moved when you jiggled them. She made all sorts of holiday creations, and then Jason and I would go out selling them from door to door after school until it got dark outside. When we were finished for the day, we'd wait under a street light until our step dad came to pick us up. While we waited, we always turned on Jason's hand held transistor radio, we each had an ear bud to listen on as Vincent Price introduced the nightly Murder Mystery Show. It had some pretty scary stories too. My brother and I stood under the safe beam of the streetlight because we knew if we dared step past the beam and into the darkness; the boogieman would surely get us. By the time, our dad pulled up we nearly jumped through the window to get in where it was safe. It seems funny today but at six years old, there was only one thing more frightening than the wrath of our mother, and that was the fear of the boogieman.

Reflecting back now, I can't seem to put a date; or year, on when I traded in my 'hero' for that ever present negative self talk (demons in my head) that seem to try and be my reality, a battle fought to this day... I long for that relationship I had with Jason.

Yes sir my friend, if you look hard enough, you too will be able to recall some of those good memories to help balance out the bad ones.

To let go of our past does not mean to regret all of it, but to embrace it by learning from it, then change what we have the power to change and start making a better history today.

Who was it in your life that you will forever be grateful to in showing you kindness amid your tumultuous life? _____

_____

_____

_____

_____

_____

_____

_____

_____

_____

_____

Start Your Own Good Memories

The book I referred to in the last chapter, 'The Power of Memories' also pointed out that if we repeat something enough, bad or good, it will stay in our memory. So I've been actively doing things for the good, and after each day, I try to take time to reflect on the positive things that took place and write them down in the 'Gratitude' section of my journal. I also change little things in my life that makes me feel better.

I never realized it until recently but I truly don't like to fold my clothes like mother taught me when I was a child because it brings back those horrific memories. It had dawned on me one day that just opening up the linen closet or a dresser drawer and seeing things folded like mother used to, always stressed me out and yet I continued to fold things in that manner because that's how it's done, that's how it's always been done.

Since I've been involved in my trauma healing now when I see clothes that are perfectly stacked it causes the hair on the back of my neck stand up, so I give the drawer a few good shakes before I close it back up... don't tell my wife I do that, okay? I now fold my towels and linens up in a roll. I even do my casual attire like t-shirts, shorts and my jeans I neatly roll them up before putting them away. It may seem silly but it's the little things in our lives, that we choose to change, that can be so liberating.

What is it in your life that you realize you do on purpose just because it's the opposite of what you had to live through? _____

_____

_____

_____

_____

TOPICS TO KEEP WORKING ON

Shame

The less we talk about shame, the more control it has on us. Keep digging deep down and share your fears, your shame, and your stories. Shame dissipates the moment you realize you are not alone.

Shame is different from guilt.

> Guilt – I did something bad
>
> Shame – I am bad

Shaming is never the solution. Feeling guilty motivates us not do the wrong again. Feeling shame paralyzes us to the point where we may take the easy way out of life, or treatment and not continue to make progress.

"Never good enough!"

Somebody put that phrase in your head and you believed it. Then you seem to have this gift of finding people who help you continue to feel that way.

Ever ask your partner what they needed and wanted, and every time you get close to meeting their needs, they move the goal post another ten feet? It may not have to do with you.

If you're a people pleaser you need to realize some people can never be satisfied. Your mom, dad, sister, friend, or spouse needs to stop looking for others to bring them happiness. Because obviously you're not up for the task. Then resentment takes hold and your no good for anybody. Don't let others take advantage of your kindness's. When someone starts taking you for granted, do what you feel you need to do, because it's true there is more happiness in giving then there is receiving. But remember "I am only one person and right now I need to take care of myself." You ARE good enough.

Before the next time you get impatient with the ones you wait on hand and foot, remember that possibly you've trained them to rely on you. You've been so efficient at taking care of them that they expect you to jump. No worries, even the oldest dog can learn new tricks. It's time to retrain everyone, including yourself. Start taking care of yourself and kindly retrain your loved ones that they'll feel better about themselves if they start doing and accomplishing things for themselves and they'll respect you in the long run.

Rejection

Men truly are no different from women when it comes to the fear of being rejected. We just have the poor ability to express ourselves, to be vulnerable. Most men really do think, "Do you love me? Am I important to you? Do you want me? Do you care about me? Am I good enough?"

Women think pornography and men have something to do with their partner's inadequate looks and or their lack of sexual expertise. Truth be told, addictions and pornography boils down to this. "For three one dollar bills and three minutes you get your needs met, and you don't have to risk rejection."

The secret is sex is truly terrifying to men. Cultivating intimacy, emotionally and physically is almost impossible when we're knee deep in toxic shame. The fear of rejection is extremely debilitating.

Life just keeps getting more crazy and stressful, that at the end of the day, we feel beat up and spit out. Now you have to put forth time and energy into your relationship so you both get your needs met. If you feel you're never good enough, or you're too lazy, then you'll retort back to the quick fix, pornography.

My friend, you're better than that, she's better than that. Invest in your relationships learn to communicate better. Strive to be a better partner, be truthful about your feelings, and dare to be vulnerable; women think it's very sexy.

Bottom line friends, relationships are hard work but if you want to stay victim free, work hard on your recovery. The better you get inside your head, the better choices you'll make in life.

Remember, it is *never* too late to change. There is a time for everything and the time to heal is now! No matter what our history, the future can bring about positive changes. We can regain self-respect and self-forgiveness, and even perhaps regain some of that dignity we seemed to have lost along the way.

-CHAPTER FIFTY NINE-

RULES in FAIR FIGHTING

All couples, partners and friends engage in conflict, resolve the conflict without being destructive. Here are some Do's and Don'ts to Fighting Fair. When you start really getting into it, remind yourself of how to fight FAIR!

<u>DO:</u>

1. Ask questions to clarify, but not judge. Never start a question with the word "Why." It puts people on the defense. Instead, use "I statements" or "Let me see if I understand… then paraphrase what they said but don't judge the words or the tone it's being said in.

2. Attack the problem, not the person. Name-calling breaks down communication and destroys trust in the relationship. Problem solving the issue together helps reinforce the power of two great minds on the same team, for the greater good.

3. Be open and honest about your feelings and what you want.

4. Brainstorm solutions. Find a happy medium there's nothing wrong with compromising Give a little to get a little.

5. Deal with one issue at a time. No playing 'Dog Pile' no fair piling several complaints into one session.

6. Deal with the Here and Now. What is the specific problem right now? Anything older than 3 days or even a week is 'History' don't bury the hatchet but leave the handle sticking out! No, "Remember you did _ _ _ _ 6 months ago?"

7. Focus on solving the issue or reaching a solution not winning an argument or ranting on how angry you are. Think win-win.

8. Give each other the ability to change their mind.

Keeping everyone's dignity in tact is always the right goal to have.

9. Give the other person equal time. The American Indians have what they called a 'Talking Stick' whoever was talking held the stick, when he was done speaking he past the stick to the other person, then it was his turn to speak. Keeping calm and patient shows respect. (Pretend you're having a Pow Wow.)

10. Go forth as equals. Remind each other you're on the same team.

11. Stick to the topic! Don't change the subject or bring in unrelated issues.

12. Limit your fight (discussion) to no more than 60 minutes. Long drawn out discussions/fights rarely reach resolution. Instead, they just wear the participants out. And when you're tired, the likelihood of doing or saying something you'll regret is much greater. If you are unable to solve your problem in 1 hour, schedule another time to continue.

13. Listen and hear! Be aware of each points of view and feelings. Try to deal with the other person's perceptions of the situation as well as your own. Be aware of his/her feelings as well as your own. Check to see whether what you heard is really, what the other person is trying to express. Much like clarifying. Also, listen with your eyes. Look at each other with kind eyes.

14. Speak softly. My wife has said to me more than once in a calm voice, "Hey, I can hear just fine. You don't have to yell." If you tend to scream when you're arguing try whispering.

15. Paraphrase what you think you heard them saying. "I understand you feel or think ...." This helps validate the other person. Mutual Validation is discussed later.

16. Take responsibility. Use "I" statements as a way to show you are taking responsibility for your own actions and feelings.

I am angry because	I hope
I am afraid	I notice
I am frustrated	I need to hear 'I love you.'
I am happier	I need to hear you're proud of me.
I am hurt	I need to hear you're on my side.
I am puzzled	I realize
I appreciate	I resent
I believe	I suspect
I expect	I want
I feel I'm being taken for granted.	I wonder

"I" statements allows you to be vulnerable and yet heard.

17. When necessary, take a time-out. It's an opportunity to restore calm and be more reflective instead of reactive. Use the time-out to reflect on why you feel the way you do and how to express yourself in a positive way. Think things through before you speak.

18. Feel patient. It's hard to BE patient, try feeling patient. Recognize the little headway your making and keep calm.

19. Timing is everything. Pick a time when you both are receptive, refreshed and in a good mood. For me, anything after 8:30pm is my shut down time, so if you want to tell me how lazy I am and I NEVER pick up after myself, probably not a good time. However, if I have a big plate of my favorite food in front of me and it's about half gone. You can tell me you wrecked the car and started a fire too close to the house in the back yard and I'd still have a smile on my face. Realistically, it's never a great time for battle, but if you keep these DO's in mind, it'll help mend things a little quicker.

DON'T:

1. Don't argue about technicalities. Avoid exchanges like, "You were 30 minutes late," "No, I was only 18 minutes late." (An easy way to distract from the issue.)

2. Don't be afraid to apologize when you are wrong. It shows you are trying. A sincere "I'm sorry" goes a long way to defuse the situation. And don't ruin an apology with a 'but.' "I'm sorry, but I still think..." Remember (**B** - behold **U** - underlying **T** - truth)

3. Don't Blame. Use "I" statements rather than "you" statements which automatically points to blame, putting the other person on the defense.

4. Don't expect your partner to read *your* mind. No, "If you loved me I wouldn't have to tell you..." (hey... "If you loved ME you'd stop thinking I had super powers.)

5. Don't interrupt or make comments while the other person is speaking. Also, watch your non-verbal expressions. Rolling eyes, heavy sighing, mocking etc. are all counterproductive...

6. Don't involve other people's opinions of the situation (e.g. "Your mom agrees with me.") The only opinions, which are relevant, are those of the two attempting to communicate at the time.

7. Don't make comparisons to other people or situations. (And "Don't take it personal, I doubt everybody!" Is out too.

8. Don't make threats (e.g., "You make me so mad I'd like to get a pencil and stick it in your neck!") Yup, I'm not making that up, someone used to say that to their loved ones. Threats back people into a corner. Tear down trust in your relationship. You may find that later you really do not want to carry out your threat.

9. Don't play games. Examples of games are; don't touch me; poor me; silent treatment; martyr; uproar; if it weren't for you...; yes, but...; see what you made me do; and if you loved me...

10. Don't read your partner's mind. No mindreading, stop your mind from trying to out-guess what they're thinking. Actively listen. If you catch yourself, mindreading say to yourself. 'Stop,

don't judge the words coming out of their mouths.' Just listen to each word and comment on those words, no matter the tone it's being delivered in.

11. Don't refer to past mistakes and incidences. Remember the 24hr, 3, or 7 day rule? It's Ancient History, let it go and move on.

12. Don't save up feelings and dump them all at once, try to air feelings often. (Remember rule #6 in the Do's)

13. Don't say "always" and "never." ("You always..." "You never...") These are exaggerations and not true, and will put the other person on the defense.

14. Don't use the following: character assassination, contempt, obscenities, swearing or taunting. Don't use sarcasm.

15. Don't walk away or leave the house without saying to your partner, "I'll be back I need to calm down." You must let them step away for a moment. I hang up the phone abruptly, and then call back minutes later. It stops me from saying things I'll regret later.

(To be honest – nobody likes to be hung up on, however it's better than an ear full of stuff you can't take back.) The point is walk away or hang up when you need to, but tell them you're coming back.

16. Do not assume, guess, imagine, take for granted, theorize, speculate, make funny glances or faces about what your partner means. Find out!

17. No finger pointing. Remember, while one finger is pointing

forward, three are pointing back at you.

18. No threatening of Divorce. In the heat of an argument, dropping the 'D' word is hurtful and manipulative. It is counterproductive and undermines your ability to problem solve. Trust is hard to restore once it is broken in this way.

19. DO NOT YELL!! No yelling, try not to yell. (Refer to the 'do list' rule number 15.)

Remember friends, dignifying others ~ dignify you.

Mutual Validation

When people don't listen to you, most often than not, the person not listening probably feels invalidated. They feel they're not being heard, so they keep up the assertions and arguments.

Validation does not mean you agree with them. It means that you understand their feelings, motivations and needs.

You get it – you understand how the other person could feel or think that way.

It's very easy to invalidate someone. While ignoring, minimizing, name-calling, and blaming are clearly invalidating, subtle things like facial expressions, body language, word choices can be equally damaging.

In mutual validation you acknowledge and appreciate their experience, you understand where they are coming from, and then you validate your own experience as well.

Example: "I understand you're concerned with... that would be hard for anyone, including me. On my end, I still feel..."

*Notice the example has two parts: "I understand..." and "On my end..." ~ that way BOTH sides are addressed.

*Accept that they have a right to their feelings that it may be reasonable to think that, others would feel the same way. That you have empathy for them. That there may be a grain of truth to what they're expressing. That they have a right to feel and think as they do, yet you have the right not agree with their point of view.

* Validating each other creates a bond between the two of you, where each person takes turn speaking, feels listened to and heard. It increases acceptance and decreases conflict. More importantly, it builds intimacy and trust, and establishes you as a respectful and safe person.

The Broken Record Technique

(The origin of the 'broken record' name is that a scratch in a (now old-fashioned) vinyl LP could cause it to repeat one section of the record time after time after time.)

When a person is trying hard to persuade, they often do not really hear your refusal. At best, they may see it just as objection that can be overcome.

When you repeat the *same words*, the pattern-recognition ability of the brain eventually notices that something is being repeated here and the other person starts to take notice of what you are saying. When they realize they are bashing their head against a brick wall, they will eventually give up (with most people, this will be quite quickly).

This is a technique to use when you are clear about what you want to say and you want this to be known. It helps you to avoid getting angry. It also helps in situations of conflict and when others are not listening to your expressed feelings, opinions or needs. It is also useful when you are asking questions for clarification or when people are trying to take advantage of you. The BROKEN RECORD is a good way to deal with people attempting to steer you away from the point, guilt tripping, and manipulation.

Example: **You** - "I need you to seat here please."

Student - "I want to seat with my friends!"

You - "I need you to seat up here please."

Student - "But I need to seat with my friends, it's really important!"

You - "I know it's important to you, but I need for you to set up here please."

YOU stay in control and not angry. Works on kids and adults alike.

-CHAPTER SIXTY-

The Mask of Anger

*I*t has taken me many years to write this book, and I have to say that Anger remains my biggest demon to control. Tara says there are still days when my fuse is shorter on some days than others. I am still learning all the time.

Remember friends, **try explaining your Anger;** learn to put words to your feelings instead of expressing your anger. When you explain your anger, you create an environment for solutions instead of arguments.

Most, if not all of us, have the gift of showing someone how mad we are. Babies and small children have feelings they can't explain like discomfort or dissatisfied they express their anger. We react by trying to calm them down and figure out how to make them happy. Sadly, Teens and adults still express their anger in such a way, people scramble around trying to figure out how to calm them down and make them happy. Slamming the door, hitting a surface hard. That's called expressing your anger. Biting, grabbing, hitting, shouting and slapping are also ways a person expresses their anger. People get the point 'yes, you're mad.' However, none of these expressions of anger really leads to a solution to what made us mad in the first place.

We need to step back from our emotions and take the time to cool down and reflect on what exactly is the underlining problem that made us mad at the start.

The only way we can make progress is to explain why we are angry, clarify the situation to figure out the exact reason or trigger for your anger. Be willing to look inside yourself to analyze what your self-talk is saying, question whether it's true or an assumption. Remember don't believe everything you think, It may not necessarily be true.

Learning to explain your anger as calmly as you can, and in a non-threatening way. Gives people something to work with. Knowledge is power, communication beings understanding. Isn't that our ultimate goal, simply to be understood?

Truly, anger is NOT a bad emotion. It's a feeling like all our other feelings. Whether we express it or explain it, it's up to you. If you choose to explain your anger, it gives others the ability to help problem solve, or at the very least, respect you enough to give you time to work it out. (If you're not willing to be mature enough to explain yourself, at least put a diaper on the next time you throw a tantrum.) That right there was funny, I don't care who ya are. Friends, try not to take yourself too seriously. Humor is a good thing, not sarcasm, learn the difference.

If you're honest with yourself, you can think of the last time you expressed you're anger then later knew you could have handled that better. Try replaying that situation again but this time **explain** what you were feeling before it went bad. Rehearse the situation so that next time you're prepared and your dignity stays intact. _____

_____

_____

_____

_____

Remember, anger is typically a secondary emotion. Here is a list of feelings that you may experience before you get angry.

What feelings are underlying our anger?

Connection / Important / Love	Control / Freedom	Dignity / Respect / Self-Worth
	Bossed around	
	Controlled	
Abandoned	Imposed upon	Ashamed
Alone	Imprisoned	Criticized
Brushed off	Inhibited	Dehumanized
Confused	Invaded	Disrespected
Discouraged	Forced	Embarrassed
Ignored	Manipulated	Humiliated
Insignificant	Obligated	Inferior
Invisible	Over-controlled	Insulted
Left out	Over-ruled	Invalidated
Lonely	Powerless	Labeled
Misunderstood	Pressured	Lectured to
Neglected	Restricted	Mocked
Rejected	Suffocated	Offended
Uncared about	Trapped	Put down
Unheard		Resentful
Unimportant		Ridiculed
Uninformed		Stereotyped
Unloved		Teased
Unsupported		Underestimated
Unwanted		Worthless
Justice / Truth	**Safety**	**Trust**
Accused	Abused	Cynical
Blamed	Afraid	Guarded
Cheated	Attacked	Skeptical
Disbelieved	Defensive	Suspicious
Falsely accused	Frightened	Untrusted
Guilt-tripped	Insecure	Untrusting
Interrogated	Intimidated	
Judged	Over-protected	
Lied about	Scared	
Lied to	Terrified	
Misled	Threatened	
Punished	Violated	

-EPILOGUE-

'Soap Box'

{By definition, a **soapbox** is a raised platform on which one stands to make an impromptu speech... The term is also used metaphorically to describe a person engaging in often flamboyant impromptu or unofficial public speaking, as in the phrases "He's on his soapbox", or "Get off your soapbox." Hyde Park, London is known for its Sunday soapbox orators, who have assembled at Speakers' Corner since 1872 to discuss religion, politics and other topics. A modern form of the soapbox is a blog: a website on which a user publishes his/her thoughts to whomever are inclined to read and or follow.}

Thank you for reading my book thus far. It's been bitter sweet to put all this on paper. It has been a battle for me to promote the reading of this book and when I meet someone who has read it, I find it hard to keep eye contact with those who have. (Good or bad, I do hope it will help you with your own journey.)

This last section I have added because of all the research and personal experience I have encountered along the way. I have cut and hacked so much trying not to sound too preachy, because hey... nobody likes to be preached to right? With that said, you are under no obligation to read further. However, if you are so inclined to continue, the following section is purely for information sake. As I attempt to stand on my little soap box, let's begin.

Beware of Being in **D**on't

Even

Notice

I

Am

Lying

"Let me tell you who's not treatable." Quoting, Rodger Smith, a therapist at an Oregon State Hospital, as he speaks on the subject of treating child molesters. "First of all, the people who continue to deny the crime. With child molesters, denial is the major thing you have to overcome... the other thing they do is they get religion in prison, which is very common for child molesters. They come in reporting born-again experiences, that all their guilt has been taken away, and that they're totally forgiven. We've got nothing to work with at this point. I think it seems to resolve all their guilt, and it doesn't' touch their fantasy structure at all." Religiosity plays a major role for anyone not wanting to face their demons properly. Religion can seem to heal their toxic shame and guilt for whatever they are trying to leave in the past. You can push an experience behind you, but it's still there, unless you learn to deal appropriately and effectively with your fantasies, impulses and your history.

Poisonous pride also plays a vital role in denial, even in conjunction with religion. God and his congregation are there to help and support. The Petra family got to the point where when someone loving came up to them and sincerely asked how things were going, they always answered,

"I'm fine, we're all good!" when clearly, the frown lines and scowl on their faces were screaming the opposite. I am reminded of that river in Egypt when I think of some of my family, we were so far into 'De Nile' that we could have been standing knee deep in that river and still die of thirst.

Regrettably, I too did the same thing. I had great teachers when it came to wearing the many isolating deceptive masks. I inherited my father's big fake smile. On the outside, I tried to be this perfect example for others to follow. However, because of my control issues, toxic anger, shame and guilt, I continually sabotaged any kind of self-worth I happened to muster up within my caustic conscience, long enough to seek help for my abusive behaviors. Through recovery, I've learned that a place of worship is not a museum for saints; it's a hospital for sinners.

I have also realized that blaming others keeps you stuck. As long as an adult child continues to blame their parents, it does not liberate them to move on with their lives, contrary to what some may think. I was talking with a friend one time, and she was going on and on about how crazy her parents were, then later she started in on how crazy her kids turned out. I turned to her and honestly told her,

"Hey, crazy don't skip a generation!"

We may not be happy about it, but because they are our family, as dysfunctional as it maybe, if we condemn our folks then we're inadvertently condemning ourselves. So, if we cannot forgive the ones who wronged us, then how can we forgive ourselves? We must accept how we were treated and move forward.

Blaming others also blinds us to the real issues. When we put all of our energy into the wrongs that our families have done to us, we lose sight on what they've done right, and what they were dealing with. Please remember, *even though we were treated tragically, we don't have to continue to live life like a tragedy.*

Part of my recovery process is making sure I'm not in denial. Denial has been such a huge part of my life for so long, that even today,

I still have to check and question my thoughts and feelings to make sure I'm not slipping back into my comfortable pair of shoes called 'Denial.'

Men Listen to Men

Men listen to men, that's why there are group recovery programs. I would assume it's the same way for women groups. Hopefully in group you'll realize that you're not alone in your struggles. You're not any different than the one you're sitting next to. If you have the guts to address your problems, and put it out there for all to see, then not only will you benefit from the instructions, but there will be at least one person in your group who will benefit from that information too.

I have never had an addiction to illegal drugs or alcohol. However, if that is (or was) part of your history, this addiction needs to be addressed. Please understand one thing. *"The consumption of drugs and alcohol is NOT the reason you committed your crime. It might have helped in your deviant act; however, a substance or liquid will never 'make you' do anything you had not already contemplated ahead of time."*

Quote from a 25 year Substance Abuse Counselor.

Always remember, you can't kid a kidder. That's the cleaned up version about making up crap and you expect others in your group to believe it. It might have worked with your victim(s) or your loved ones but when you're in-group, Keep it real, tell the truth, eat another piece of humble pie, and continue to grow.

People with the least self-control are the most controlling people.

I feel the need to express my thoughts on just how out of control some perpetrators are. My opinion on the extreme need for them to be removed from the house and away from not only their victim, but also their secondary victims too. By secondary victim, I mean the adult in the perpetrators household. The one not involved in the crime, the one left picking up the pieces.

While I was incarcerated, I can't tell you how many times I'd see an inmate on the phone with their spouse literally screaming at them because they didn't answer the phone when the inmate called three minutes earlier. Or they'd go on and on about how they were, 'the boss and you need to do this and you need to do that.' It always amazed me how the inmate was still trying to have power and control over their loved ones. Perpetrators truly need to have some down time, to process what they did. But more importantly, if not for them then it would give the innocent victims enough time to stop and regroup, because most perpetrators put themselves in the position, where the family depends on his income, possibly the only source, making it seem impossible for victims to come forward. So although hard, it would give the spouse enough time to stop buying into the lies of the perpetrator and realize that they CAN do for themselves, they CAN think for themselves. That they CAN in fact regain their own power and control over themselves. In turn, they can finally start living life free from the perpetrator, if that is what they choose to do, even if they decide to stay, if the spouse can just not answer the phone when she is being bullied, she will finally see that she's worth more than her incarcerated husband or ex-husband will ever realize. Nobody deserves to be cussed at, yelled at, or made to feel worthless. By dignifying others, you dignify yourself.

Trust Issues

For those of us who are in need of trauma healing, trusting in your recovery process will be very hard but not impossible. Many have failed to complete the program, for numerous reasons. Some have never fully recognized the severity of their crime. Others simply don't invest the time or energy it takes to do the program correctly. Many are stuck on their supposed rights, sorry but you forfeited any of those rights the moment you committed your crime, and chose to abuse.

Your victim may be your primary, but you cannot forget about the many secondary victims: Your family, your victims' family, along with friends, workmates, schoolmates, and the legal system (with that said, anyone who has your life in their hands, they can figuratively be considered a god; yes, your caseworker, probation / parole officer is god. Make the gods happy by doing what you're supposed to do. They are not there to make you comfortable; they're there to help you succeed.) Your therapist is not trying to trip you up, their teaching and challenging you, to help you grow. It is not their fault you're failing, it's you it has always been you. If people would spend half that time, they do in their thinking errors, 'victim stance'/ 'uniqueness' and more time figuring out, 'Okay, what am I doing wrong, what am I not getting with this.' Honestly, talk to the people who have your life in their hands, plea with them to help you help yourself. Trust in the process, buy into the program, there are thousands of success stories. Some of us truly do stand in our own way of making life a success, in group or otherwise.

(I know, "Hey this dude never had MY councilor!" Once you've re-picked up this book from throwing it. Just remember were ALL on the same team. Everyone involved in your life wants you to get better, to be better, and to make better life choices. A therapist once said to me in passing, "You know sometimes I envy the ones in group. Once we help you tear down all those unhealthy walls and poisonous coping skills, you have a clean slate to rebuild a new foundation, a new beginning.")

Post Traumatic Stress Disorder Treatment

PTSD treatment started out primarily for those involved in the military. Now in recent years PTSD has expanded into civilian life where sadly, some homes can be considered war zones. Anyone who is having problems with processing a traumatic experience in their life, whether it was a car accident or a death of a loved one, a rape, or abuse of any kind, you owe it to yourself to seek out a PTSD Treatment program in your area.

Psychotherapy, or counseling, involves meeting with a therapist. There are different types of psychotherapy:

*   Cognitive behavioral therapy (CBT) is the most effective treatment for PTSD. There are different types of CBT, such as cognitive therapy and exposure therapy.

*   One type is Cognitive Processing Therapy (CPT) where you learn skills to understand how trauma changed your thoughts and feelings.

*   Another type is Prolonged Exposure (PE) therapy where you talk about your trauma repeatedly until memories are no longer upsetting. You also go to places that are safe, but that you have been staying away from because they are related to the trauma.

*   A similar kind of therapy is called Eye Movement Desensitization and Reprocessing (EMDR), which involves focusing on sounds or hand movements while you talk about the trauma.

Remember me telling you about Tara saying I have a short fuse some days, most days? I've learned, for me, I have a problem with trying to 'mind read' Tara. Whenever she would say anything, even just as innocent as asking me how my day was, I would misinterpret it and think she had ulterior motives and I'd snap at her. Someone living as if they had to 'walk on eggshells around me' is not living, and not fair. When I realized I had picked up that survivor's skill of 'mind reading' as a child along with my trust issues, I began to see it was ME who had been sabotaging my relationships. So now, I actively have to tell myself, not to judge the sentence that was just spoken to me, and to reply only to those words, no reading anything else into, and answer how I would like to be spoken to.

I can tell you also that for as long as I can remember, I have slept on my stomach, which as you might know is bad for your body and breathing. However, it's the way I've slept to protect my body from the blows of the Hot Wheel track and mother's rage. Coming in and beating us in the dead of sleep, was exhausting. Going through PTSD treatment, I can honestly say I now catch myself waking up in the morning on my back! I can't explain it but my mind has healed enough to allow my body to relax to the point that I'm able to sleep properly. You cannot make this stuff up.

That barely touches on what I've been learning. Please, seek recovery for your trauma healing.

Along with coping and self-esteem skills, I've learned through my PTSD treatment, one-on-one and in-group. My life continues to be more meaningful and my relationships more rewarding. I am humbled and yet grateful for my instructors and their patient and non-judging, informative sessions.

References and Recommended Reading

"Humble and Grateful Acknowledgements to the following (in order of use...)"

'By Silence Betrayed'   by John Crewdson 1988   ISBN 10: 0316160946

'Facing Codependence'   by Pia Mellody 1989   ISBN 0062505890

'I Got You Babe.' Song by Sony and Cher. 1965

'When Acceptance is Denial' by Gil Ericksen 1993   ISBN 10-0963886878

'A Child Called It'   by Dave Peltzer 1995   ISBN 1558743669

'Adult Children of Abusive Parents' by Steve Farmer 1990   ISBN 978-0-345-36388-6

'A fine line-When Discipline Becomes Child Abuse'

                              by David A Sabatino 1991   ISBN 0-8306-3566-1

'Necessary Losses'   by Judith Viorst 1986   ISBN 10:0-684-84495-8

'Bradshaw On: The Family'   by John Bradshaw 1990   ISBN 978-155874427-1

'The Resilient Self'   by Steve J Wolin and Sybil Wolin 1993 ISBN 978-0-8129-9176-5

'The Child Within'   by C.L .Whitfield 1987   ISBN 0932194400

'If Only My Family Understood Me'   by Don Wegscheider 1979   ISBN 10: 0896380386

'The Power of Memories'   by Frank Minirth 1995   ISBN 978-084077641-9

'Better Boundaries'   by Jan Black and Greg Envus 1998   ISBN 10:1572241071

'Adult Children as Husbands, Wives, and Lovers'

                              by Steve Farmer 1990   ISBN 0-929923-21-1

'Homecoming'   by John Bradshaw 1990   ISBN 0-553-5793-6

'Healing the Shame That Binds You' by John Bradshaw 1988   ISBN 0-932194-86-9

*Original poem 'To Me' from the book '**I Remember Myself**' (The Journal of a Survival of Childhood Sexual Abuse) by*

Laura Donaforta
P.O. Box 914
Ukiah, Ca. 95482
$8.00 includes the postage

www.jamestpetra.com Reviews and Comments are welcome or for more books. Give me your address in an Email, and or have someone else send me your address, time permitting I'd be honored to hear your **healing** story. Very possibly for a second book.

Whether you're part of the free world or in a gated community.

~ GROUNDING ~

Grounding is a set of simple strategies to detach from emotional pain (like anger and sadness). Distraction works by focusing outward on the external world, rather than inward toward the self. You can also think of it as "a safe place," "centering," "distraction," "healthy detachment," or "looking outward."

WHY DO GROUNDING?

When you are overwhelmed with emotional pain, you need a way to detach so that you can gain control over your feelings and stay safe. Grounding "anchors" you to the present and to reality.

Many people with PTSD or those people, who are struggling with feeling overwhelming emotions and memories or those feeling numb with dissociation, benefit from grounding. In grounding, you attain a balance between the two: conscious of reality and able to tolerate it.

Guidelines

*Focus on the present, not the past or future.
*Grounding can be done any time, any place, anywhere, and no one has to know.
*Keep your eyes open, scan the room, and turn the light on to stay in touch with the present.
*Note the grounding is not the same as relaxation training. Grounding is much more active, focuses on distraction strategies, and is intended to help extreme negative feelings. It is believed to be more effective than relaxation training for PTSD.
*Grounding puts healthy distance between you and these negative feelings. Use grounding when you are faced with a trigger, enraged, dissociating, having a craving, or when ever your emotional pain goes above 6 (on a 0-10 scale).

WAYS OF GROUNDING

There are three major ways of grounding, comfort, mental and physical.
"Comfort" means talking to yourself in a very kind way.
"Mental" means focusing your mind;
"Physical" means focusing on your senses (scent, sight, sound, taste, and touch);
You may find that one type works better for you, or all types may be helpful.

Comfort Grounding

*Plan a safe treat for yourself, such as a snack.
*Remember the words to an inspiring poem or song.
*Remember a safe place. Describe the place that you find so soothing.

*Say a coping statement: "I can handle this." Or "I am safe now; the trauma is in the past."

*Say kind statements, as if you were talking to your child within - for example, "you are a good person going through a hard time. You'll get through this."

*Think of favorites. Think of your favorite color, animal, season, food, time of day...

*Think of things you are looking forward to in the next week- perhaps a visitor is coming, or calling home.

Mental Grounding

*Describe your environment in detail, using all your senses-for example, "The walls are tan; there is a table and chair; there are sounds of people laughing..."Describe objects, sounds, textures, colors, smells, shapes, numbers, and the temperature. You can do this anywhere.

*Play a "categories" game with yourself. Try thinking of singers or musicians, types of Cats, states that begin with M...

*Say a safety statement. "My name is_____; I am safe right now, I am in the present, not in the past." "I am safe now, I'm okay."

*Say the alphabet, or count to 10 very s...l...o...w...l...y.

Physical Grounding

*Breathe in a scent not related to your trauma.

*Dig your heels into the floor-literally "grounding" them! Notice the tension centered in your heels as you do this. Remind yourself you are connected to the ground.

*Eat something, describing the flavors in detail to yourself.

*Focus on your breathing, notice each exhale and inhale. Run cool or warm water over your face or hands.

*Hold a small stone, shell, piece of wood touch and look at it.

*Jump up and down

*Listen to calming music.

*Notice your body: the weight of your body in the chair; wiggle your toes in your socks; the feel of your chair against your back...

*Stretch. Roll your head around; extend your fingers...

*Walk slowly; notice each footstep, saying "right" or "left"...

GROUNDING DOES WORK! However, like any other skill, you need to practice, practice, practice.

You can do this, DON'T GIVE UP!

ABOUT THE AUTHOR

James T. Petra grew up on the west coast and now lives in a small town in the mid-west with his wife Tara. To date, he is still active in P.T.S.D. treatment and motivates others to share their healing story, encouraging them to also stop wearing Too Many Masks.

"Friends, it's hard being the 'poster child' of what NOT to do while I went through life before Trauma Healing and Recovery. As I encourage people to read my book, once they finish reading it, I find it hard to make eye contact with them. However, it's nothing in comparison to the years of bottled up toxic shame and emotional baggage I've lived with all my life. To live through such horrendous abuse then to continue the cycle of abuse, is mind boggling, until you see my thought and feeling process. It by no means justifies my actions as a perpetrator; it does however, shed light as why I made the choices I've made. Adult children of abuse must get help; we cannot break this cycle on our own. Please, I urge anyone who reads this to get the help you need and deserve. We can stop the cycle of abuse, one voice at a time." *JTPetra

Petra / Too Many Masks

www.ingramcontent.com/pod-product-compliance
Lightning Source LLC
LaVergne TN
LVHW051459080426
835509LV00017B/1817